Removing Your Shame Label

LEARNING TO BREAK FROM SHAME AND FEEL GOD'S LOVE

EDDIE CAPPARUCCI, LPC, CSAS

BLACK ROSE writing™

First printing

ISBN: 978-1-68433-010-2
PUBLISHED BY BLACK ROSE WRITING
www.blackrosewriting.com

Printed in the United States of America
Suggested Retail Price (SRP) $17.95

Removing Your Shame Label is printed in Minion Pro

DEDICATION

To my Lord and Savior Jesus Christ, who always had me in His sight and His hand on my shoulder even during those times when I turned away from Him due to the shame of my brokenness. I thank Him for giving me the opportunity to Finish Strong.

To my amazing wife Teri, who saw the man I could become before I saw him. I appreciate her dedication, sacrifice, and endless love. To my children, Chelsea and Dakota, who helped melt my heart of stone and provided me with so many wonderful and memorable moments that I will forever cherish.

To Rev. Dr. Bob Bullock, who guided me in understanding the importance of developing a deep and meaningful relationship with my Lord and Savior Jesus Christ.

To Rev. Dr. Timothy Erskine, who taught me to attempt to live every moment in the Spirit and not the world. I also thank him for seeing my potential as a Christian counselor.

To Rev. Dr. Timothy McConnell, who continued to assist me in my sanctification journey and taught me how to move out of my comfort zone. Today, he still serves as a dear friend.

To John Speiser who was always there to offer encouragement and to assist me during my Spiritual journey, especially during those times when I felt lost.

To Rev. Aaron Moore for his contribution in developing an inspiring and meaningful Forward for this book.

And finally, to Rick Sloss whose eagle eyes assisted in making this book stronger and whose dedication to prayer is aimed at the desires of God's heart.

Removing Your Shame Label

"What a wretched man I am! Who will rescue me from this body that is subject to death? Thanks be to God, who delivers me through Jesus Christ our Lord! So then, I myself in my mind am a slave to God's law, but in my sinful nature a slave to the law of sin."

Romans 7:24-25 NIV

"Then I shall not be put to shame, having my eyes fixed on all your Commandments."

Psalm 119:6 ESV

FORWARD
BY REV. AARON C. MOORE

When I was a twenty-year-old college student I found out I was getting a new brother. My mom called one day and said, "I need to talk to you". I said "sure". But she said, "no, I want to come up to the college to talk to you". This sounded ominous, but of course I agreed. My mom and dad hopped in the car and drove the hour and a half from Charlotte to Gardener-Webb University where I attended… to "talk".

We began by walking down to the campus pond. It was a beautiful day, but I was anxious with curiosity. Finally, we stopped by a bench and my dad with all the tact he could muster said, "well dear, spit it out". My mom began to cry. My first thought was that she was sick, and they were here to tell me she was terminal. Mom caught this direction that my mind was going without a word being said. She said, "no, it's good!" Ok, at this point I could think of only one thing that would cause my parents to drive an hour and a half to "talk" to me. "Are you pregnant?" I asked. I was the youngest of 3 brothers and twenty years old, so my folks were not spring chickens. They began to laugh hysterically, and then my dad through his laughter said, "kind of". At that point, my mom began to tell me a story about her past through more tears.

When mom was my age she became pregnant. The father was not my dad. My Paw-Paw was a hard man and the shame that this behavior would have brought on their family would have been too much to bear, so they thought. He sent her to a special home in Charleston, SC for young, pregnant, unwedded teens. She put the baby up for adoption in 1968 and never had any further contact with the child or the future parents and only told two people outside her family – my dad, and her best friend.

Fast forward to 1998. No longer a baby, but now a thirty-year-old man sent my mother a certified letter that he would like to meet her. The rest is history. On that sunny day around the pond I learned I had another brother. It was a beautiful story-book ending; a Hallmark plot really.

But for thirty years this inspirational journey was a dark cloud of *guilt* and *shame* that hung over my mom every morning and every evening. It wasn't until she came to this process of reconciliation with my brother that she could be set free from her shame label. The ironic part was that her story was so inspiring. Her courage to give birth to my brother was a bold move in her time and the shame she carried for those thirty long years could have been healed long before this final reunion took place.

The book that you're about to read is full of stories like this of people who walk through life with a label of shame that often has been self-placed. And even in the times when shame *seems* to be the appropriate response, it's not a label anyone needs to, or ever should carry for thirty years.

This is a book of healing; a roadmap to comprehensive health for your thoughts, emotions, and actions. Not only is this book helpful in dealing with our own shame, but it's a terrific resource for understanding the paths that our friends, family, coworkers, and fellow church members walk. When we understand shame, we grow in our compassion for others.

Eddie's insights in this book, is like the navigator voice on your GPS telling you when to turn left or right, how many miles to the destination, and the occasional instruction to make a U-turn. The ultimate destination is Christ.

At one-point Eddie asks the question, *"Would you feel ashamed if someone could read your thoughts? Well, God can."* And while that thought might fill us with fear, it's because our understanding of how Christ sees our past is not ordered correctly in our thinking. We've veered off course. Eddie calls on the resource of Scripture, pastors, and theologians from all walks to help us grasp God's great affection and call for us to trust His Word.

Removing Your Shame Label will help you understand your past, how it effects your present, and how getting that truth lined up with the truth of Christ will affect your future. The roadmap that is being laid out in this book is one that will lead you to find the truth of how God sees you in Christ. It will help you find your center, your self-worth, and your loveliness in the eyes of the one that matters most; the one who made you and loves you with an everlasting love.

TABLE OF CONTENTS

1. Introducing the Christian Shame Cycle 10
2. The Shame of Impure Motives 34
3. The Shame of Carrying Garbage 43
4. The Shame of Staying Stuck 58
5. The Shame of Being Distracted By Distractions 78
6. The Shame of Contaminated Thoughts 88
7. The Shame of Loving with Conditions 103
8. The Shame of Uncontrolled Pride 111
9. The Shame of Excessive Worry 125
10. The Shame of Self-Loathing 135
11. The Shame of a Hardened Heart 145

CHAPTER 1: INTRODUCING THE CHRISTIAN SHAME CYCLE

"Does your shame label prevent you from experiencing all of God's love? You are far from alone in suffering from this relationship-eroding disease."

"When will it end?" Tony asked with tears streaming down his face. "I have no idea how to get control of it." He was talking about his eating disorder. At the age of 29, Tony carried 330 pounds on his 5' 9" frame. He had never been in a relationship with a woman and only had one friend who lives several thousand miles away. His weight, combined with an inactive social life, leaves him feeling lonely and depressed.

All of this has severely impacted Tony's self-worth. "Even though I try to dress nice, I feel like a slob. When I look at myself in the mirror, I want to get sick."

A financial analyst, Tony had struggled with weight his entire life. "I had been fat since I was a child," he said. "Now look at me. Years later, and I'm still out of control. The frightening thing is I can't imagine it ever changing. I will be like this until the day I die."

You may find it heartbreaking as you listen to Tony outline his struggles with obesity, but it is even more troubling to hear him express the shame he carries.

"I call myself a Christian, but is this how a Christian should act?" he asked. "I just can't say no to food. Gluttony is a sin, right? But I am telling you, there is nothing I can do about it. You would think as a Christian I would have more self-respect; I have none! I'm a pathetic waste!"

Tony's shame depletes his self-esteem, while leaving him with a sense of emptiness. What does emptiness feel like for Tony? It feels like God is disappointed and has abandoned him.

"When I sit in church, I sense people are staring and making comments about my weight," he continued. "I sit there feeling very alone. But not just because I feel others are rejecting me, but because I feel God is rejecting me."

Emotionally moving stuff, isn't it? What Tony is demonstrating to us is the intensity of his "shame label" due to his out-of-control behavior. Worse yet, because of his shame, he is convinced God has written him off and refused to acknowledge him.

While your own struggles may be different, can you relate to Tony's story? Perhaps, some choices you've made leave you feeling inadequate, insignificant or stupid. Do you question God's love and commitment for you? Are you worried God has turned away, embarrassed by your actions? Does your shame label make you feel unloved? If so, you're far from alone.

"You are probably surrounded by Christians who feel shame. You are far from alone."

Although you may not realize it as you sit in church on Sundays, you are more than likely surrounded by like-minded Christians who also struggle with shame because of their self-defeating, even sinful, lifestyle and how they believe God views them.

Take me for example. As a young Christian in my 20s and 30s, I struggled with sexual integrity issues. I was a womanizer. While it did not stop me from going to church every Sunday, it had a negative effect on my relationship with God. How would I describe that relationship? Basically, I felt it was non-existent.

I thought my sins were too ugly for God to deal with. I remember thinking, "*why would my Creator put up with the nonsense I engage in? He must look at me and wonder, Where did I go wrong with Eddie?*" There is a saying God doesn't make junk. Whenever I heard someone say that, I thought to myself, "*Well, He made one piece of junk – me.*"

You see, just like Tony and many other Christians, I was harboring shame. While I admit I enjoyed the sinful behavior I was engaging in; I hated myself for doing it. I could not understand how I lacked the self-control just to say no. I also was under the false assumption other Christians had mastered the art of resisting temptation. So why was I different? What was it about me that made me such a bad person?

Today, as a Christian counselor, I see similar pain in many of my Christian clients, who struggle to manage their wrongful behaviors. They feel trapped in an endless cycle of emotional turmoil, worry and hopelessness. It is a cycle that ultimately results in the development of a "shame label" they wear, as well as a belief that God has rejected them.

What Is Shame?

Now let's stop for a moment and make sure we understand the true definition of shame. Many people confuse shame for guilt – but the two are very different. Have you ever felt bad about lashing out at someone? We all have. That's guilt.

Guilt is an emotion we feel when we realize we have done something bad: "I should not have said that to Susan. It was wrong of me." Guilt deals with the act we have committed.

"Guilt condemns our sinful actions.
Shame condemns us."

Shame, on the other hand, takes our guilt to a deeper, more self-deprecating level. Shame attacks our inner being by hammering guilt into self-condemnation: "I can't believe I talked to Susan like that. Once again, I've demonstrated what a moron I am when it comes to dealing with people. No one should ever want to be my friend."

Shame doesn't focus on the act committed; it focuses on *you*, the individual who committed it. From my personal experience in both living with shame and counseling others, I've come to believe shame is the most destructive of all emotions; if not kept in check it can destroy a person's self-worth.

When we are engrossed in shame we play the destructive game of comparing ourselves to others. What this does is intensify our shame as we embrace the perception other Christians around us have their acts together. We perceive them to be very much at peace, while we hide and wallow in our private sin.

Tony's shame was compounded when he compared himself to those he deemed "good" Christians, who sat in the pews with him on Sunday. In comparing himself to other Christians, who he perceives as righteous and pure, Tony concludes that he doesn't belong. "When I go to church I feel like an outcast," he told me. "I can't even focus on the sermon or the service. I am too distracted by the negative thoughts running through my head. My thoughts tell me to get the hell out of there because I should not be around these good people. I do not deserve to sit among them or call myself one of them."

Two Lies

For Christians like you, Tony, and me, it comes down to two key issues that keep us in painful emotional distress. And they are two of Satan's strongest lies designed to keep us feeling trapped.

Lie #1: *Our "performance" is the measuring tool God uses to judge us. Therefore, we must eliminate all sin from our lives and be pure and righteous Christians.*

When we fail to live up to this impossible goal, our shame label grows larger due to our inability to "get it right".

Lie #2: *God can never accept or love anyone who struggles and/or repeatedly engages in sin. He wants no part of us until we become "good children".*

This leaves us feeling unloved and unwanted by our Creator. We think of ourselves as outcasts who have been rejected by our Heavenly Father.

These torturous thoughts are promoted by Satan to keep us stuck on a negative, emotional rollercoaster of self-doubt. There is no sense of peace – only perpetual worry God no longer favors us because despite the fact we once accepted His Son as Savior, we are not keeping Christ as Lord of our lives. Thus, we are "bad" people.

Some of my clients tell me this endless struggle keeps them out of the church pews. They feel inferior to those around them. Have you ever experienced similar feelings during your time at church or around Christian friends? Does it seem as if others know you are harboring a secret?

The Devil's Wedge

Even if these shame-ridden believers are in the pews and hearing about God's love, they believe it is a message they're not worthy of embracing. Many pastors focus on delivering a consistent message to their flock that growing in relationship with Jesus Christ is vital to their Christian walk. And they are correct. However, Christians who bear the shame label due to continual sin have a difficult time with that message. Their shame prohibits them from being honest with Christ about their struggle and from cultivating their relationship with Him out of fear of condemnation and rejection.

"It's pretty difficult to turn to God in prayer and worship after you had just finished intentionally vomiting your dinner," said Caroline, who is working on overcoming a severe eating disorder that causes her physical distress. "You know you are acting in a way that Jesus would not like, so how do you approach Him? I just can't bring myself to be honest and remorseful with Him because, I'm so ashamed for destroying my body."

The shame label is one of Satan's most powerful and effective tools.

Like Caroline, many of us who engage in sinful behaviors find it difficult to take the actions necessary to strengthen our relationship with Jesus. Shame is a self-maintained barrier between us and our Lord. It limits our ability to engage in meaningful prayer, scripture reading and Christian community. It's difficult to pray to someone who you believe is judging you as a failure. It's difficult to read about and appreciate the Father's unfailing love when you believe your sinful patterns disqualify you from His love. It's difficult to interact with Christian brothers and sisters when you feel unworthy to be around them.

The shame label is one of Satan's most powerful and effective tools that he utilizes to drive a wedge between good people and their God. He uses our shame to blind us to the truth about our sinful nature and His grace, and to generate feelings of worthlessness because we fail to exhibit self-control. Satan draws on our shame to prevent us from seeking God and making things right with Him, therefore, denying many of us the wonder of experiencing His complete love and presence in our lives.

Believing God Has Abandoned Us

We are left believing God has turned His back on us, but the truth is shame has stopped us from engaging in the relationship, confessing our shortcomings, and embracing His grace and forgiveness. It is the fear that He will judge us as "bad" and reject us because we can't manage our sinfulness. However, what we fail to recognize is God is not attaching the shame labels to us – we are attaching them to ourselves. We are projecting onto God how we think and feel about ourselves – as failures and disappointments. That is not how God sees us.

I refer to this as the Christian Shame Cycle.

Christian Shame Cycle

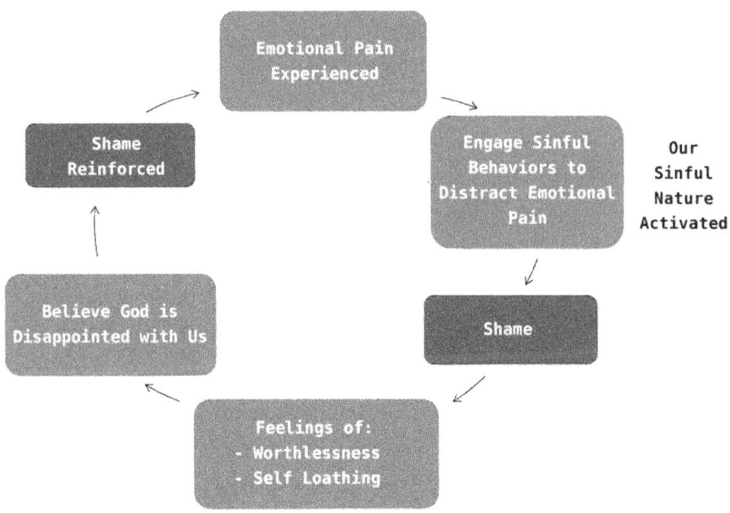

"When I was sitting in church last week, I got that familiar feeling I was inadequate," said Carl, a social worker who struggles with chronic depression. "It seemed in my mind that everyone around me was a good, sin-free Christian. They seem so happy and alive. It seems they are joined at the hip with God. But that is not how I feel. God ran away from me a long time ago."

Carl is one of many Christians trapped in the Christian Shame Cycle. What is this cycle?

We enter the Christian Shame Cycle when we experience an event that brings us emotional pain. The pain can range from simple boredom to the complex breakup of a long-term relationship. It is this emotional pain that leads us to act out – usually in some type of sinful manner – in order to distract attention from the distress and soothe ourselves.

Our misguided response may be to withdraw from others, not giving them an opportunity to nurture us. Or we may turn to excessive pleasures that will monopolize our time and take our mind off our emotional discomfort. This could be using food to soothe, excessive shopping, endless video games or television. Still, we may find ourselves turning to addictive and more-destructive behaviors including alcohol, drugs and illicit sex. Whatever sinful activity we elect to indulge in the result is the same. We end up ashamed of our actions.

Once shame engulfs us, we are moving along to the next step in the Christian Shame Cycle, where we experience negative self-talk and feelings of worthlessness and self-loathing. We become our worst enemy as we flog ourselves for not being able to "get it right".

At that point, we take our internal negative thinking and project those destructive feelings about ourselves onto God. We believe He is disappointed with us and has turned His face away from us. We tell ourselves, "*There is no way God could love a fool like me. I am sure He thinks of me as a failure*".

And what is the result of the negative and internal beating we administer on ourselves? It reinforces the shame label. We then sit with that shame until the next event occurs that inflicts emotional pain, and we will begin the cycle again.

The Christian Shame Cycle is not the work of God. It is self-induced and endorsed by Satan. We were designed to be perfect creatures; however, Adam and Eve changed that and instead we became enslaved to sin. But our desire as believers in Christ is to be obedient children of God by the power of His Holy Spirit. And when we fail to allow God's Spirit to do so – which we will – we experience shame that drives a wedge in our relationship with Him.

Please pay close attention to this point. It is critical to understand when we feel distanced in our relationship with God, it is not His doing. We intentionally widen the relationship gap because we are too ashamed to stand before Him and admit that we are weak, vulnerable and sinful. We want to hide our faces as Ezra did when he discovered the Israelites had been marrying into neighboring tribes that paid tribute to other gods and idols.

He was too embarrassed by the sin of his Jewish brothers to approach God in humble contrition: *"I am too ashamed and disgraced, my God, to lift up my face to you, because our sins are higher than our heads and our guilt has reached to the heavens"* (Ezra 9:6, NIV).

"When we feel distanced in our relationship with God, it is not His doing."

Just like Ezra, we become so disgusted with our wrongful behavior that we can't contemplate how God would want to have anything to do with us. This, in turn, can preclude us from engaging in prayer, worship, and fellowship.

"I have gotten to the point where I am withdrawing from people at church," said Cheryl, who has a problem with shoplifting. "As I sit among them, I feel so out of place and alienated. If they knew what I have done, they would have nothing to do with me. They are all good, Godly people – the opposite of me."

What Cheryl does not understand is that all of those "good, Godly" people battle daily with their own sinful nature. While most may not act out in the way Cheryl does, they are just as guilty of violating God's law in one way or another. If Cheryl could conduct a survey of the sins committed by her peers she would be shocked at the results.

Individuals like Cheryl have bought into the notion that those sitting in the pews or in her Bible study or prayer group must all be faithful and loyal disciples of God. Perhaps they are, but that doesn't mean sin is not a struggle for them. Sin is a struggle for all of us. It's the result of what occurred in the Garden of Eden when Adam and Eve fell.

In order to break the Christian Shame Cycle, we need to have information based on truth and logic and not our misperceptions, such as the one presented by this client of mine:

"I find it hard to believe He wants anything to do with me," said Emerson, a college student who is struggling to keep his virginity. "He knows the ugly thoughts that go through my head 24/7. God doesn't want to deal with a pervert like me who undresses girls with his eyes!"

Can you see how frustrated and tortured Emerson is by his thoughts? The truth is his thinking is incorrect. Let's examine the reasons why his thoughts go against everything that God represents.

We Are All Sinful

All of us suffer from a sinful nature. It is a universal aspect all humans share – we are sinful creatures. No one escapes this reality. Not you. Not me. Not anyone.

"Indeed, there is no one on earth who is righteous, no one who does what is right and never sins." (Ecclesiastes 7:20, NIV)

When you ignore this biblical principle, you subject yourself to unnecessary guilt and shame. There is a drowning in emotional pain that leads to increased negative thoughts and feelings of worthlessness. As time goes on, you find yourself sinking in an emotionally negative cesspool with a shame label that is difficult to peel off.

Do you believe we should be able to control our sinful behavior? Well, it would be beneficial if we would be more aware of our actions and try not to engage in impulse behaviors. But we are not robots. As much as we may try we can't always control how we act or react in any given situation.

Danger of Being Drained

This is especially true when we find ourselves mentally, emotionally, physically or spiritually drained due to numerous internal and external factors that we face on any given day. Think about when you are feeling hungry, angry, lonely, tired, run-down, or bored. Would you say that you are thinking clearly during those times? Indeed, you're not. That is because your mind and body are focused on what is draining you.

"When you are mentally, emotionally, physically, or spiritually drained, bad things happen."

When we are depleted of our emotional, mental, physical and spiritual resources, we are more likely to react poorly to outside influences that we perceive are making our lives more difficult. My wife will tell you not to think about engaging me in a meaningful conversation after 10 p.m. Why? Because at that time of the day, I am feeling drained and talking is not at the top of my to-do list.

Now, if you want to be brave and attempt to engage me at that hour, you most likely will get a very limited response and my "what are you thinking" face, which will leave you feeling neglected. That outcome would not be my intent. Had you engaged with me earlier in the day, you most likely would have received a different and more positive response. Because we are more likely to be reactive when drained it is important for us to be aware of our mental, emotional, physical, and spiritual states. When we are cognitive to the fact we are depleted, we can gently warn others that "now is not a good time".

Granted, some people's sinful nature is more active than others. But why are some individuals more prone to engage in negative thinking, emotions, and behaviors? There are numerous reasons, but the environment in which we were raised and the role models who taught us how to give and receive love are major contributing factors.

If you were raised in a culture that promoted and encouraged the giving and receiving of emotional intimacy, then you are more likely able to better handle the emotional pain and stresses of life that can lead to sinful behaviors. If instead, you were raised in a home in which drama, abuse and neglect were the norms, you will find it more difficult to manage and ignore the triggers that can lead to sin.

Whatever the reason for our acting poorly, our sinful nature puts us in direct violation of God's natural design for love and trust. Since that moment in the Garden of Eden, men and women have been inflicted with a never-ending hunger to have their selfish desires fulfilled. Part of our flawed human nature is a primitive drive for self-indulgence and attention, which we often attempt to fulfill at any cost. For millennia, men and women have committed deplorable acts to obtain what they desire – murder, theft, and slavery are a few examples. But what was the catalyst to these actions in the first place? It is our sinful nature.

In the heart of every man and woman on earth is darkness. This darkness consists of thoughts and emotions that are self-centered and, when acted upon, prove to be hurtful or harmful to others. There is not a man or woman who can honestly say they have not succumbed to their sinful nature. It is part of our brokenness as humans.

Add the bombardment of media messages you receive each day that entice you to act inappropriately. This is one of the core problems facing us today. More than ever, today's society calls you to become more inwardly focused. It screams out:

- Seek satisfaction of your wildest desires
- Tell people exactly how you feel about them
- The only one who matters is you
- The one with the most toys wins
- If it makes you happy or feels good, do it
- Don't compromise
- Don't rely on anyone

It is difficult enough to maintain control over our sinful nature without the endless parade of images depicting lust, greed, pride, gluttony, and envy that are pushed upon us daily. The world is constantly telling us everything is permissible. There is no right or wrong. This serves to excuse, justify, and exacerbate our sinfulness.

Even if we have the best intentions our minds become cloudy when exposed to temptations on a regular basis. Our "filters" clog and our best judgments lapse. We find ourselves acting out in an impulsive manner without pondering the consequences. We can become so lost in our thoughts that we sometimes are oblivious to the evil and deceit that lies within our own heart.

No one has the market cornered on sin. It is a burden all of us must bear – whether we are walking fully in the light of God or in the shadow of darkness.

God Doesn't Abandon Us

"Come now, let us settle the matter," says the Lord. "Though your sins are like scarlet, they shall be as white as snow; though they are red as crimson, they shall be like wool." (Isaiah 1:18, NIV)

How can it be God can love us when we display sinful disobedience? The answer is Jesus Christ. In Jesus, we are not only saved from the condemnation of our sinful nature, but we are also free from our shame.

Do you doubt that?

Remember earlier when we looked at the mindset behind our struggle with sin? We pointed out one of our beliefs is our "performance" is the measuring tool God uses to judge us. We struggle in our attempt to put forward a "good" performance because we erroneously believe we do not measure up to God's expectations.

"The only performance that matters is what Jesus Christ did at the cross."

But guess what? We are looking at the wrong performer! God's love and acceptance of us has nothing to do with our performance. The only performance that counts is what Jesus obediently endured when He went to the cross. It is His performance that allows our sins – past, present and future – to be forgiven. It is His performance that brought us back in alignment with God. It is His performance that empowers our future and empowers us to remove our shame labels.

"When he had received the drink, Jesus said, 'It is finished.' With that, he bowed his head and gave up his spirit." (John 19:30, NIV)

In my heart, that is the most powerful verse in the Bible. It was Christ who, in going to the cross, allowed us the wonderful opportunity to walk in the presence of our God. It was His performance, and His alone, that allows for us to hold our heads high even though we are broken due to our sinfulness.

Our own "performance" means nothing when it comes to receiving God's love and acceptance. It is our decision to accept His amazing gift of grace that bonds us to God. Nothing more and nothing less. In fact, those of us who struggle to deal with sin are correct about one thing: we never, ever will "measure up" or "be good enough" to win God's love and earn salvation on our own.

Our sinful flesh and hardened hearts make that impossible to achieve. But once we accept God's loving and breathtaking grace we can rest in knowing He will never abandon us.

"The LORD himself goes before you and will be with you; He will never leave you nor forsake you. Do not be afraid; do not be discouraged." (Deuteronomy 31:8, NIV)

God Is Ever Faithful

Is it difficult for you to believe God is forever faithful even when you are not? Is it impossible to wrap your mind around His amazing, remarkable, unconditional love? Then you are one of many Christians who are trapped in the Christian Shame Cycle.

We are going on a journey through these pages that I hope will help you break free from that cycle and grasp the depth of God's love and commitment to you.

"And hope does not put us to shame, because God's love has been poured out into our hearts through the Holy Spirit, who has been given to us." (Romans 5:5 NIV)

I get chills up my spine whenever I read that verse. Imagine a part of God Himself and His love being placed *within you.* Do you love that way? Could you love that way? I know I struggle to love as God does.

Why do we struggle to love God and feel His love toward us? Because we buy into the shame label that has been thrust upon us, while doing a lousy job of acknowledging His Holy Spirit within us. God can't and won't abandon us.

He is in us! If we are feeling distant from God, it is because we are the ones responsible for creating the separation.

God doesn't move away from us because of our sin nature;
we move away from Him.

Our sinful nature is what results in our shame and impacts our ability to seek God's direction, guidance, understanding and love. God doesn't move away from us because of our sin nature; we move away from Him. And when we move away from God, we have difficulty feeling His love.

"All of us like sheep have gone astray; each of us has turned to his own way." (Isaiah 53:6 NIV)

When we are wrapped in shame, we prefer to live in the dark instead of the light. Why, because it is easier to hide in the dark. The light is bright and brings all things into focus, which leads us to feel more shame as our transgressions are exposed for all to see. Therefore, we prefer to remain in the dark hiding with our secrets. It feels safer there because we do not have to expose our fears. But in reality, it is not safe at all. What we are doing is handcuffing ourselves, limiting our ability to express our love to God and feel His love toward us. Instead, we experience a sense of emptiness that comes when God is not the focal point of our lives.

But when we can lift ourselves out of the darkness and walk into the light we allow ourselves to be joined in Spirit with God. When this happens, it leads to one of the greatest gifts He offers us – inner peace with Him and the freedom to love ourselves and others again. His Spirit gives us this power.

One Source of Inner Peace

Are you one of the many people in this world who struggles to obtain inner peace? Do you long to escape the endless worry and the numerous burdens the world brings every day? Are you tired of wearing your shame label? Do you have any idea where to find such a sense of peace?

There is one true and sustaining source of inner peace and freedom that each of us can tap into. And it comes from being involved in a vibrant relationship with God. In fact, He promises it: *"Peace I leave with you; my peace I give you. I do not give to you as the world gives. Do not let your hearts be troubled and do not be afraid."* (John 14:27)

But to achieve peace we must stop looking negatively at ourselves and instead see in us what God sees. We must begin the process of removing our shame label. God doesn't think we're ugly; we think we're ugly. We must also come to the realization that God is with us in the form of the Holy Spirit. As believers, it is our inability to focus on and rely on the Spirit that leaves us with a nagging void that can never be satisfied until we come to acknowledge our need for God in our lives. Then He is glorified.

The Holy Spirit never weakens. He is always powerful and a source of strength to all of us. *"But I say, walk by the Spirit, and you will not carry out the desire of the flesh. For the flesh sets its desire against the Spirit, and the Spirit against the flesh; for these are in opposition to one another, so that you may not do the things that you please. But if you are led by the Spirit, you are not under the Law."* (Galatians 5:16-18 NIV)

"We ignore the Holy Spirit when we position ourselves at the center of life."

The Holy Spirit is our source of strength, but we must learn to embrace Him. We ignore the Holy Spirit when we position ourselves at the center of life. We ignore Him when we become preoccupied with our day-to-day routines. We ignore Him when we are paralyzed by fear. We ignore Him because of our shame. We ignore Him when we develop the "I can do it alone" mentality. Soon, we become islands unto ourselves, despite having God's Spirit within us. And the nagging void continues to grow.

We suppress the Holy Spirit when we neglect to feed our soul with God's Word, being in prayer, spending quiet time seeking His voice, celebrating in worship and being in authentic relationships with others. When we neglect these essentials the nagging void continues to grow.

Removing the Shame Label

You have read this far so my guess is that you struggle with shame, which has led you to believe God views you in a negative light. Maybe you're wondering, *how do I get off this toxic merry-go-round that leaves me feeling unloved, unwanted and empty?* In these pages you will find the answers you seek, including:

- Hope in learning you are not helpless in the battle with sin
- Relief in realizing your shame is self-created and is not how God views us
- Comfort in realizing your performance (being perfect and sin-free) is not the way to God's heart
- A renewed sense of belonging when you discover the truth of God's love and His promise to be faithful to you
- A sense of freedom and peace-of-mind that can be found when you understand the magnitude of God's love and grace
- An understanding of what God really ask of us (to repent our sinfulness and yield our hardened hearts to His forgiveness and grace)
- A roadmap of proven Christian teachings and counseling exercises that will assist in successfully managing sinful behavior – thus removing self-induced shame and transforming your heart

You are going to learn Jesus loves to break the Shame Cycle!

Your Roadmap to Thinking, Feeling and Acting Differently

This feature at the end of each chapter provides biblical and psychological guidance for managing your sinful nature and eliminating shame.

- **Avoiding Satan's Traps**
- **Asking for God's Help**

- **Turning to Others for Guidance**
- **Identifying Your Blessings**

1. Avoiding Satan's Traps

How can you better abide in God's Word and resist temptation? Stay the heck away from Satan and the traps he sets for you every day! Unfortunately, he is a champion deceiver, tempter, and accuser. And his objective is simple: expand the wedge in our relationship with God and others.

Christian author and scholar C.S. Lewis describes Satan's cunning maneuvers: "*What Satan put into the heads of our remote ancestors was the idea that they could 'be like gods' - could set up on their own as if they had created themselves . . . Invent some sort of happiness for themselves outside God, apart from God. And out of that hopeless attempt has come nearly all that we call human history - money, poverty, ambition, war, prostitution, classes, empires, slavery - the long terrible story of man trying to find something other than God which will make him happy.*"

In turn, when we move away from the path of Christian maturity and instead, attempt to feed our own selfish and sinful desires, we are playing right into Satan's hands. When we question whether God loves and accepts us, we allow Satan to take a stronghold in our lives. We buy into one of his many lies designed to bring emotional misery and keep us apart from God.

In order to keep Satan at bay, we need to move away from worldly values and make it our objective to live by God's values. What do His values look like? Well, we need to look no further than the virtues the Apostle Paul outlines in Galatians 5:22. He called these the Fruit of the Spirit.

To help ourselves stay on paths of purity, we should aim to measure all our thoughts, emotions and actions against the standards of love, joy, peace, patience, kindness, goodness, faithfulness, gentleness, and self-control. Any desire of the heart that doesn't align with these virtues is one we should question and cast out if it will ultimately cause us to sin.

Write these virtues on a 3 x 5 card and place them in a location where you will see them each morning. (I have them in a picture frame mounted on the wall in my home office.) Spend time each day reviewing each virtue individually, taking a moment to determine what it means to you. Meditate on how living each of these Godly virtues to the fullest can positively impact your life. For these are God's gifts to you.

Then make a commitment to bring the Fruit of the Spirit to life in your daily thoughts and actions. As you encounter various circumstances throughout the day, see which of the virtues you can tap into to enhance the situation. Over time, you will sense that these Christ-like virtues are becoming part of your personality and way of life. When that happens, not only will you experience richer relationships with others, but you will enjoy more intimately the love and presence of God in your life.

2. **Asking for God's Help**

Becoming in tune with the Holy Spirit requires us to be involved in continuous self-reflection, to identify our weaknesses. Three or four times a year, conduct an inventory of your faults (pride, untamed tongue, lustful eyes, etc.) on a sheet of paper and bring them before Christ. Let Him know how weak you are in each of these areas and that you need His strength to change.

"Do not be afraid to share your brokenness with God."

Do not be afraid to show God your brokenness. Do not allow your shame to keep you from sharing with your loving Father the pain and suffering you endure due to your sinful desires. Instead, understand that He knows your brokenness and will not judge or condemn you when you come before Him with a humble spirit. *"If you confess your sins, he is faithful and just to forgive you your sins"* (1 John 1:9). Trust Him to lift you up and demonstrate how His love can help you move away from the sinful trap that ensnares you.

Pastor and author Rick Warren writes this about our weaknesses: "The truth is, God created you with weaknesses. And, since He's God, He couldn't have made a mistake. Is it possible He created you with weaknesses to keep you on your knees before Him? With you dependent upon Him, you're able to do all things through Him who strengthens you."

God understands there are circumstances in our lives we can't manage on our own – we are not strong enough. He wants us to lean on Him for guidance and direction. He doesn't want us to try this alone. And He doesn't want to be an assistant. As Hubie Mann, former director of Christian Education at Eastminster Presbyterian Church in Marietta, GA says, "He wants to drive. So, move over and let Him. In fact, don't sit in the passenger seat or the backseat, instead get in the trunk and let Him lead the way for your life". In this way, God is glorified and not us.

Over the following weeks and months, through discernment and meditation (quiet time), evaluate your progress in curbing your sinful nature. In those areas where you continue to fall short, bring them to Christ again and ask for His strength and wisdom. Be sure to update your self-reflection inventory on a regular basis. In fact, don't be afraid to seek input from family members and friends on where they feel you can improve. Wow, how's that for being vulnerable!

3. Turning to Others for Guidance

Need additional help in managing your sinful nature? Then seek accountability. A very helpful way to get control of a sinful behavior is to reach out to trusting individuals with whom you can share your struggles. Remember, part of the issue regarding our sinful nature is that we keep it hidden in the dark from others. By bringing forward the sinful desires we hold onto, we expose them to the light and God can work it for good.

One of my clients was a 17-year-old female, who escaped the emotional pain of a troubled home by seeking the attention of older men. For a period of nine months, she engaged in promiscuous behavior and ended up contracting a venereal disease – which fortunately was cured with proper medical care. She had grown up in a church-going family and attended Christian schools. Now, she wanted to know how to break her habit of promiscuous behavior and deal with the shame of her tarnished reputation.

After spending several months working through her emotional pain, she stopped acting out sexually. We then began the process of removing the shame labels she had created as part of her new identity. Part of this included understanding she now was in possession of a powerful testimony she could use to assist other teenage girls struggling with sexual sin. This empowered her with a new sense of self-worth and purpose. After leaving for college, she went on to volunteer at community centers that assisted troubled young women in getting their lives back on track. She exposed her sins to the light, and God used her to shine as a light for others in need. *"But everything exposed by the light becomes visible – and everything that is illuminated becomes a light"* (Eph. 5:13-14).

By admitting our weaknesses, we are removing the stranglehold of sin in our lives. Our sins are no longer secrets. These heavy rocks –comprised of fears, insecurities, scars, loneliness, abandonment, addictive behaviors, hatred, neglect and more – can be removed from our tote-bag.

Dietrich Bonhoeffer, a Lutheran German pastor who was killed by the Nazis days before the end of World War II, had this to say about confessing our sins to others: *"Why is it that it is often easier for us to confess our sins to God than to a brother? God is holy and sinless; He is a just judge of evil and the enemy of all disobedience. But a brother is sinful as we are. He knows from his own experience the dark night of secret sin. Why should we not find it easier to go to a brother than to the holy God? But if we do, we must ask ourselves whether we have not often been deceiving ourselves with our confession of sin to God, whether we have not rather been confessing our sins to ourselves and also granting ourselves absolution. . . Who can give us the certainty that, in the confession and the forgiveness of our sins, we are not dealing with ourselves but with the living God? God gives us this certainty through our brother. Our brother breaks the circle of self-deception. A man who confesses his sins in the presence of a brother knows that he is no longer alone with himself; he experiences the presence of God in the reality of the other person."*

Sharing our sinful secrets with others helps rid us of dependency on our sinful desires. It helps us start the process of shedding our shame. But a word of caution: Make sure the person or persons you select to share with are reliable, trustworthy and safe.

4. Identifying Your Blessings

I have never been a great fan of one positive-psychology technique, in which people are encouraged to stand in front of the mirror and repeat over and over how special and unique they are. That approach seems rather shallow to me (although I will admit there are other beneficial techniques in the theory of positive psychology). The idea I can become happy by talking to myself positively goes against my deeper-evaluation approach to therapy. However, during a sermon at the church I attend one Sunday, our pastor, quoted C.S. Lewis as saying, *"It is a Christian's duty for everyone to be as happy as he can."*

"It is a Christian's duty for everyone to be as happy as he can." –C.S. Lewis

---

Those words stuck with me as I pondered the circumstances faced by most of my clients. Nearly all of them have a difficult time seeing pass the negativity that impacts their lives. They struggle trying to understand that solutions exist and that their emotional pain can be eliminated.

When working with married couples, it is not unusual for me to show them the drawing below, which consists of numerous dark clouds with the word *Negatives* written over them. This is most likely how they view their relationship. They see all bad and nothing good. Nearly every couple agrees with this assessment.

It is human nature for us to focus our attention on circumstances going wrong in our lives, instead of seeing and enjoying the positive events and

circumstances that surround us. That's sad. More importantly, it's wrong.

As Christians, we need to develop a moment-by-moment practice of focusing on God's blessings, faithfulness, and never-ending love. You may have heard the expression, "Each day is a gift from God," but we are not naturally good at opening that gift and sharing it with others. Appreciating all God does for us – even if it is simply the basics in life – lead us to develop freedom from pain, misery, and sin.

After showing couples the image of the dark clouds, I explain how we tend to focus on negativity because it is what seems to fall within our line of sight. However, during troubling times, we often don't recognize the many blessings in our lives because they sit out of our line of sight. Look at the next image.

Our blessings are there – we just can't see them. Why? Because we are too focused on what is *not* going right in our lives. We can have nine things going well for us, but if one thing is out of sorts, we focus our attention there, spending endless energy and time obsessing over the one element that isn't lining up properly. This dampens our mood and steals our joy.

I realize there are times when it is difficult to find the blessings in our lives. But even when things seem hopeless, there is hope in our relationship with Jesus Christ.

Remember Tony at the beginning of this chapter? After coming to the belief that he was not capable of disappointing God, and understanding his worldview of fellow Christians was incorrect, Tony was able to begin the process of removing his shame label. He came to understand why he had trouble controlling his appetite and realized he used food since he was a teenager to comfort the emotional pain of watching his parents' endless fighting. Although he moved out of the house to attend college, he had taken with him the shameful habit of gluttony.

But with this new insight into his behavior, Tony went to work on learning mindful eating and began an exercise regimen for the first time in his life. He lost 45 pounds. More importantly, he came to understand that he is the child of a King and that his performance – whether positive or negative – will never change that fact.

Removing your shame label requires breaking the Christian Shame Cycle. It means believing that you are unconditionally loved and accepted by your Heavenly Father, despite your human flaws and sinful nature.

And once you embrace this new belief, you'll discover an amazing and powerful inner desire to abide by His wishes and commands.

Now here is where the hard part comes. As humans, we are caught in a battle between our spiritual (new) self and our flesh (old) self. It's time to examine some of those battles and how they play out in our lives. But more importantly, let's look at the steps we can take to win more of those battles, break the Shame Cycle, strip away the label of shame, and embrace the authentic, intimate relationship God wants with us.

Bottom Line: Is Our Objective to Live Sin-Free?

The simple answer is no. Our sinful nature is a direct result of what transpired in the Garden of Eden. Even if we do not sin through our behaviors, it remains in our nature. We can never be sin-free in this life.

So, what is the bottom line for us when it comes to sin?

God understands we are and will always be sinful creatures in this life. Therefore, He sent His only begotten Son to remove our sinful burdens through His action on the cross. That leaves us free from the worry and shame of sin. What God asks of us is that we place our hand in His, trust Him, and begin the journey of allowing Him to transform our hearts. This is called sanctification, which is the process of becoming Christ-like. But we do not do it on our own – we need God's Spirit.

As author and pastor John Piper writes: *"One of the reasons I am the kind of Christian I am, with the theology that I have, is that I know the Bible requires of me things that I cannot myself immediately produce by my own power. I am fallen. I am sinful. And yet, I know I should be feeling the emotions the Bible expects me to feel. I know myself guilty."*

I tell my clients who battle sexual addiction, "The fact you are learning to hate the sin is a step in the right direction. Your heart is changing. And that is the key to learning to live a new life in Christ. We allow our hearts to be transformed and we learn to live in the Spirit."

We begin this journey the day we accept Jesus as Savior. Think of it as God saying to you, *"I can't wait for you to have the opportunity to see yourself as I see you – a perfect creation I designed. You will get the chance on the Day of Judgment, but for now, walk with me and abide in my Son, so that you can start to see for yourself just a small glimpse of what Christ-likeness looks like while you are still here in this world."*

CHAPTER 2: THE SHAME LABEL OF IMPURE MOTIVES

"Almost every sinful action ever committed can be traced back to a selfish motive. It is a trait we hate in other people but justify in ourselves."

—Stephen Kendrick, The Love Dare

"Motive" is one of my favorite words. Webster's dictionary describes motive as "a need or desire that causes a person to act". You cannot follow a court case without someone trying to determine a motive. Determining the motive when a crime is committed is essential in ensuring a conviction. But motives also play a critical part in our lives.

Each day you make hundreds of decisions. If you think about your decision-making process, you would probably conclude that decision-making has become a routine. Often, decisions are something we do not put much thought into. These are minor decisions such as "what to wear", "what to watch on television", "what route to take to work today" and "what to eat" (unless of course you live in my house). We refer to these decisions as habits.

Other decisions are major and require us to take more time to discern. Decisions such as: whether to take a new job; move to a new city; change churches; or whom to marry. In some cases, we struggle to make decisions out of fear. The thought of taking the wrong action can frighten us to the point of leaving us feeling paralyzed. It can become so strong we make no decision at all. This is called analysis-paralysis. Yet, in other circumstances, we are so desperate for change that we make snap decisions that we later come to regret.

That is why when it comes to decision making, we must lean on the word "motive". Depending upon our motive, the course of action we select can range from 'proving to disapproving'; 'smart to stupid'; or 'caring to insensitive'.

In our haste when making a decision, we tend to lean more toward reacting based on worldly values rather than using Spiritual values. This of course often leads not only to poor behavior, but also to feelings of regret and guilt in knowing that we could have handled the situation much better.

Well-known pastor and author, A.W. Tozer in his book, *The Pursuit of God* said, *"It is not what a man does that determines whether his work is sacred or secular, it is why he does it. The motive is everything. Let a man sanctify the Lord God in his heart and he can thereafter do no common act. All he does is good and acceptable to God through Jesus Christ"*.

"It is not what a man does that determines whether his work is sacred or secular; it is why he does it." –A.W. Tozer

---

In our decision-making process, there are two motives driven by our sinful nature that we use to justify most of our actions.

- ☐ It will allow me to indulge in self-gratification
- ☐ It will allow me to impress others with my self-worth

As we discussed earlier, today we live a society that demands instant gratification. We can find truth in this all around us. Take texting for example. Before cell phones, there was no expectation that communication with others would be instantaneous. Years ago, someone would call and if you were not available they would leave a message and expect you to get back to them when you were available. Today, the expectation is if you receive a text message you will respond immediately. And if you don't you may end up with a series of text message such as:

Where are you?
I just sent you a text.
Did you not get it?
Are you ok?
Are you mad at me?

Hello?!!!!

I hate you!!!!

Actions taken with the purpose of self-gratification involve impure motives. They are actions centered on ourselves and designed for one purpose – to have it our way. This type of behavior occurs when we become disconnected from our hearts. This tends to put all the emphasis on us and none of it on others. We become inwardly focused as opposed to being outwardly focused. This approach flies in the face of God's teaching and desire for our lives.

"Do nothing out of selfish ambition or vain conceit. Rather, in humility value others above yourselves not looking to your own interests but each of you to the interests of the others." (Phil. 2:3-4)

Our sinful nature of self-gratification leads us down a path where we find ourselves indulging more in the pleasures of the world than in the wonders that can strengthen our relationship with God and others. When we take that path, we are turning away from God because the focus is on what we want. It is very difficult to over indulge in selfish pleasures and simultaneously feel we are close to God. In fact, I would say it is impossible.

Pastor and leading author Chuck Swindoll in his book *Day By Day,* had this to say about what occurs in us when we are following the path of engaging in impure motives. *"If you listen long enough you will be tempted to throw your faith to the winds, look out for number one, let your glands be your guide, and choose what is best for you," he says. "Initially you will get a rush of pleasure and satisfaction, no question. But ultimately you will wind up disappointed and disillusioned."*

Personally, I have found during times when I am internally focused, I missed out on numerous opportunities in which I could have connected and shared with others. When I am self-absorbed I pass by those who could use my assistance; I fail to recognize others' achievements and milestones; I miss out on engaging in meaningful fellowship; I fail to demonstrate to others the difference God makes in my life; I am more impulsive and lacking self-control; and I am incapable of sharing God's love. We can understand why acting on our sinful nature draws us away from God. But remember, it is us who are drawing away, not God.

Acting to impress others is another form of impure motives that can lead to poor outcomes. You have heard the term "keeping up with the Jones" well, that is how many of us live. We are constantly comparing ourselves and our lifestyle to those around us. We find little in the way of contentment with what we have, which drives us to achieve and acquire more "stuff." We become obsessed with the thought of being looked "down upon" by others. This leads to decision-making that is deeply rooted in sinful and impure motives and can be costly in many ways, including living beyond our means. It also can generate actions that end up tarnishing our reputation and name.

I recall a young mother in one of our Sunday school classes being very vulnerable and admitting how she had got caught up in that lifestyle, especially when it came to her children.

"Children's birthday parties in our neighborhood became huge events with one mother trying to outdo what the last mother had done," she told us. "I remember when time came to plan my 6-year-old daughter's party, I spent more time focusing on what would impress the other mothers rather than on what my daughter wanted in a party."

She is not alone. Attempting to impress others is based on our desire to feel valued, accepted and wanted. This takes us down the performance mentality path. This is not uncommon among children who feel they must earn their parents' love. Their goal becomes to impress their parents through their academic and extra-circular activities.

"Taking action to impress others is another form of impure motives that can lead to poor outcomes."

What they are seeking is their parents' approval, attention and acceptance. In many cases, this behavior continues as they become adults. Whether it is their spouse, children, or boss, they still believe it is only through their positive performance people will accept them. Eventually, many discover the hard way they are only as good as their last performance.

Once you have trained people to accept you because of your ability to jump through hoops, they expect you to keep jumping. Such a lifestyle can leave you feeling drained and resentful. And when the day comes that you can't keep up, (and that day will come) you are left feeling inadequate and like a failure.

I recently came across this comment on a discussion board encouraging people to try and impress others. *"Live loud and proud. Being unashamedly who you are and letting your passions in life shine through is very impressive to people, even when they don't realize it. Everyone wants to live like they don't care what others think, so when they see someone doing that, they are impressed."*

Really? I thought we referred to these types of individuals as "obnoxious."

The God Answer to Changing Our Impure Motives

Is it possible to serve God with wrong motives? Absolutely. How many of us have agreed to take on a church project because it was highly visible and ensured we would be noticed? My hand is raised. Paul points out in 1 Tim. 6:3-10 how false teachers use financial gain in teaching the Gospel.

"But God will reveal our true motives. "...He will bring to light what is hidden in darkness and will expose the motives of men's hearts" (1 Cor. 4:5).

When it comes to decision making how do we ensure our motives are true and not based on our sinful nature? There is one simple question we can ask ourselves before we make any good intentioned decision. "Is what I am about to do being done for God's purpose and Glory?"

"Am I now trying to win the approval of human beings, or of God? Or am I trying to please people? If I were still trying to please people, I would not be a servant of Christ" (Gal. 1:10).

To help us answer these questions we should turn to the Holy Spirit to assist us in discerning truth and wisdom in our decision making. The Holy Spirit can provide us with insight and comfort in knowing that our actions glorify God. Yet, for many believers, the Holy Spirit is a mystery they claim they have not experienced. But Scripture tells us otherwise.

"Where shall I go from your Spirit? Or where shall I flee from your presence? If I ascend to heaven, you are there! If I make my bed in Sheol, you are there! If I take the wings of the morning and dwell in the uttermost parts of the sea, even there your hand shall lead me, and your right hand shall hold me"

(Psalm 139:7-10).

As believers, there is no escaping the reality of the Holy Spirit. But as I ponder the thought of "God within us," it does make me pause. While there is no doubt, I often feel the presence of God within me via the Holy Spirit. I know there are times, especially those in which I become reactive to negative circumstances that I lose sight of a special gift that can help me direct my thoughts, emotions, and behaviors.

When we are having difficulty feeling the presence of the Holy Spirit it is not because He is absent. The Spirit has not left us. We have trouble experiencing Him because we are not cognitive of Him in us. We are so wrapped up in our own self-indulgence or too occupied with worries that we don't tap into this amazing gift God has given us. The gift of God Himself! With God in us we can experience peace even in the most difficult of circumstances.

As believers, we must always remember we are filled with the Holy Spirit - it is God within us. However, we also must remember as humans we are easily distracted and allow outside influences to lead us to react to situations in ungodly ways because we don't turn to the Spirit for the power, wisdom and direction it can provide.

Your Roadmap to Thinking, Feeling and Acting Differently

- **Be Cognitive of the Reality of the Holy Spirit**
- **Engage in On-going Self Reflection**

1. Be Cognitive of the Reality of the Holy Spirit

With all the busyness around us, it is very easy to slip back into chasing worldly values and moving away from Spiritual values. It is my belief many of the decisions we make are put forth without any thought. We just "do it". Have you ever seen someone throw a cigarette out the window of their car when driving? Do you think most people are thinking to themselves *"this is littering, and I should not do it, but I am going to do it anyway"?* I doubt it.

We walk around with so many thoughts running through our heads at one time that we make hundreds of decisions each day without giving any thought to them. And some of the decisions — while seeming to be innocent

— are less than good ones. Have you ever grabbed something to eat on the run, woofed it down and only after you are done eating said to yourself "why in the world did I eat that"? It probably happens more times than not. We act without thinking.

The key to making positive decisions and ensuring our motives are pure is maintaining awareness of our thinking. But more importantly is in maintaining the awareness of "God with and in us." By staying cognitive of the fact, we are children of the living God and He wants to work through us to demonstrate His purpose and Glory. In that way we set ourselves up to make successful decisions. And in case you missed that important point I just made, let me repeat:

He wants others to see His light shining through our eyes. He wants others to look with amazement when we sacrifice our time, money and talents to help those He draws to us. Not for us to get the credit, but for Him to get the credit. However, for that to happen we must be aware God is with us via the Holy Spirit.

"God wants to work through us for His purpose and Glory."

One of the best ways to remain cognitive of God's presence is to ask this simple question before taking any action — "what is my motive?" You will find out that there are three potential answers to that question:

- ☐ I am trying to gain self-gratification
- ☐ I am trying to impress others with my importance
- ☐ I am trying to walk in God's purposes

If you're certain your decision is for God's purposes and Glory you're on the right track and have made a good choice.

Another way to remain aware of God's presence is what I call "God 24/7." With this approach, we engage with God throughout the day by taking time to reflect on Him and His promises. It may be a 15-second prayer; listening to a Christian song; reading a short Biblical verse; giving a shout of praise; admiring nature; checking in on a friend, holding a door open for someone; giving a warm-felt hug; or listening for God's direction.

The list of examples is endless. But the point is to keep God foremost in your mind throughout the day. You will find out this approach leads to decision making based on pure motives that bring a sense of warmth and peace in both good and difficult times. We make focusing on God a regular habit, instead of only engaging Him when we are looking for His help and comfort.

"The practice of God 24/7 increases your awareness of His' presence and never-ending love."

If you begin the practice of God 24/7, it becomes a new way of life, and you benefit by experiencing the presence of God with you always. It not only increases your joy, but it lessens your sadness, frustration and worry. It ensures pure motives.

2. Engage in On-Going Self Reflection

Part of the process of living in the Spirit is making a commitment to engage in self-reflection on a regular basis. This self-evaluation measures where we are in our effort to allow Christ to take the lead in our lives. It is very easy to get drawn off course in our attempt to follow Christ. Therefore, it is critical we are always honest with ourselves about our thoughts, emotions and behaviors and where we are falling short in our Spiritual walk.

Self-reflection is a painful process because it opens our eyes to our sins and can leave us feeling inadequate and shameful. It can also help us realize we have reached a point in our journey in which we are stuck in our Spiritual pursuit. Self-reflection assists us to understand our shortcomings and points out to us temptations we should avoid. Finally, the process enables us to see what we are chasing in life including the false idols we create and pursue.

I dislike going through self-reflection phases because I know I need to be completely honest with myself, and when that happens, I have to confront the ugliness that lies within. Although I may try to convince myself I have it all together and that I am a great example of transformation, the more I look within the more I continue to find flaws and defects in my character. And they are not new. They have been there for a long time and I have done a good job keeping them hidden from others as well as myself.

For example, I have a difficult time reconciling when someone does something that I find hurtful or hurts someone I know. I often have a tendency to "write off" people very quickly. Although I have gotten somewhat better, it is still a struggle and I am not always very good at turning the other cheek.

But this does not keep me – and should not prevent any of us – from looking in the mirror on a regular basis and making an accurate assessment of our lives and our sinful nature. If we don't take on this exercise we run the risk of declaring ourselves righteous and pure, which is an outright lie. We open the door for Satan to convince us we can be god-like. It opens us up to become rebellious and worst yet to inappropriately judge others by outward appearances. When we say we are without sin, we are lying to ourselves, others and God.

"If we claim to be without sin, we deceive ourselves and the truth is not in us" (1 John 1:8).

Get out the Windex™, clean off that mirror and start peering into the window of your heart and soul. Take time to check the true reading on your motive gauge. Your search can begin today.

CHAPTER 3: THE SHAME IN CARRYING GARBAGE

"If you don't have peace, it isn't because someone took it from you; you gave it away. You cannot always control what happens to you, but you can control what happens in *you." -John Maxwell*

Believe it or not, many of us go about each day followed by a foul smell, and no matter how many times we bathe or how hard we scrub it doesn't come off. It is a smell that emits toxic odors in the way of negative thinking, shaming feelings, and inappropriate behavior. That horrid smell is *our past.*

Nearly all of us have been tainted by negative influences as we were growing up. There are the pains of abandonment, neglect and abuse that even though they occurred years ago still haunt us. There are also events from our childhood, adolescent and teen years that resulted in constant anxiety and emotional distress - family violence, divorce, death of a parent, serious illnesses, bullying, homelessness, learning disabilities, and natural disasters that we can't shake off.

I provide my clients who have experienced trauma with an image of them carrying a garbage bag over their shoulder. It's a bag they have been carrying throughout life. It not only contains hurts and wounds of the past, but it continues to grow in size and weight from current shameful thoughts, feelings and behaviors. With the additional weight comes enormous problems such as depression, fatigue, addictions, and physical illnesses. The contents of the bag become our shame label.

Todd was in his late 20s and a recovering crack addict when he came to see me. Growing up in the northwest, he came from a family of artists and loved music. After college, he was hired to perform with a symphony. Todd had been a quiet and reserved child who earned good grades and rarely got in trouble. However, when he was 8, Todd was sexually abused by an older boy in his neighborhood. This abuse went on for several years with the older boy making threats to keep Todd quiet. The abuse stopped when the older boy went off to college, but by that time, Todd was carrying an emotional garbage bag – his shame label.

Due to the abuse, fear became a constant in Todd's life. He became afraid of everything and was extremely guarded around people. Todd had created a worldview that "people can't be trusted and will hurt you if they can get away with it." Worse yet, Todd developed a shame-filled soul. He would spend hours reliving the abusive acts and torturing himself for being so "weak" for not fighting back and for submitting to the wrong that was done to him. He even questioned whether he was to blame for the abuse.

Over time, Todd began to withdraw and isolate himself from others. Because he did not trust people, he made no attempt to befriend others; he focused solely on school, work and music. This trend continued throughout college and even as he started his career as a musician. However, the loneliness was catching up with him.

One day after rehearsal, he saw several musicians huddled together, smoking crack. They invited him to join them and he did. Todd never looked back. He loved the feeling getting high gave him – a sense of calm and peace. Smoking crack made his fears and shame label disappear but only until the high wore off.

Over the next few years, Todd relied heavily on drugs to soothe himself. But with the calm that came through drug use, other harmful issues started to arise. His addiction was driving him into debt, and he started missing rehearsals. Eventually, he lost his job and he ended up slipping deeper into isolation. His shame label had not been alleviated; it had only been reinforced.

How It All Begins

More than anything else, children long for security. Think about it: kids can't fend for themselves. They need adults to provide food, shelter, and protection. And with that, they require nurturing and attention. Children want to believe their caregivers are a trustworthy source of comfort and will provide for their many needs. When this does not happen, and a child finds himself in an abusive or neglectful situation, he begins to experience high levels of anxiety because he feels unsafe.

When trapped in this constant state of negative over-stimulation, the child's anxiety becomes the norm. After a while, he barely recognizes he is anxious. The child/teenager knows something is not right but he learns to physically and mentally handle the intense anxiety level by developing coping mechanisms that serve as a comfort source.

"When trapped in a constant state of negative over-stimulation, anxiety becomes the norm in our lives."

Pornography, excessive masturbation, drugs, alcohol, food, shopping, video games, and even watching endless television can all be sources of comfort for a child or adult.

On the other extreme, activities such as cutting, hair pulling, and skin picking all can help reduce high levels of stress by serving as distractions. The garbage bag that originally was filled with painful memories of abuse and neglect now becomes packed with additional guilt and shame over the use of unhealthy coping mechanisms.

As a young girl, Sally experienced an ongoing physical and verbal abuse from her mother. Her father, a passive man, would stand by and do nothing to protect his daughter from her troubled mother. However, once the abusive episode was over, Sally's father would take her out for something to eat to cheer her up. Over time, Sally began to equate food as a source of comfort whenever she experienced emotional pain. By the time she reached middle school she was extremely overweight, which led to excessive teasing and bullying.

Not feeling protected at home or in the classroom, as a teenager Sally later turned to alcohol and promiscuous sex to numb herself. She carried these coping mechanisms into her adult years. It was here she came to think of herself as an "out-of-control" woman who had no willpower when it came to food, alcohol or sex.

It wasn't until she entered counseling that Sally came to realize her behaviors were unhealthy tools she used to protect herself against the emotional pain she had been repressing for years. She also was able, for the first time, to view her father not as a concerned parent but as an enabler who made matters worse by inadvertently teaching her to use food to soothe her pain during times of stress.

Sally's garbage bag contained not only the abuse she had suffered at the hands of her mother, the failure of her father to protect her, and the rampant bullying she had endured, but also the shame and humiliation of her food, alcohol, and sex addictions. What started out badly for an innocent young girl continued to turn tragic for her as an adult.

Even King David recognized we could carry negative events that befall us in our youth with us into adulthood. *"Greatly have they afflicted me from my youth, yet they have not prevailed against me. The plowers plowed upon my back; they made long their furrows"* (Psalm 129:2-3, NIV).

David tells of the deep scars we bear due to the abuse and neglect of those whom we may have trusted. But for many, these are not yet scars; they are open wounds that are yet to be dressed and healed. These wounds remain sensitive and still ooze. The results of our wounds show themselves in different ways through destructive thought patterns and behaviors. Worse yet, the poor behaviors that result from our wounds often spill out onto new, innocent victims.

Roderick and his wife, Nancy, came to see me after she discovered pornography on his cell phone. Married for three years and the parents of a 1-year-old boy, they have struggled in their marriage with Nancy complaining that Roderick had a difficult time expressing his emotions.

"Our wounds from the past spill out and negatively impact innocent people around us."

During one-on-one sessions, Roderick outlined an extremely abusive and neglectful childhood. When he was 5, his mother would take him when she went to have sex with strange men. When he was 7, his mother eventually left him and his father. His father, bitter and angry over his wife's infidelity and abandonment, did not tolerate Roderick expressing any feelings and would beat him if he would complain about anything. His parents had given him a heavy garbage bag to carry – a shame label – at such an early age.

Over the years, Roderick created an erroneous worldview that emotions were bad and should not be expressed. He also discovered pornography at a young age and used it as a distraction to soothe the pain of his mother's abandonment and his father's rigid rules.

When they entered counseling, Nancy knew little of Roderick's past. She had thought of him as quiet and reserved, but also as a good provider and faithful husband. But Roderick's garbage bag spilled out onto Nancy in his betrayal with pornography and his inability to emotionally bond with her. The garbage bag he had been carrying leaked out into his marriage and had strained the relationship with his wife.

Unhealthy coping mechanisms developed in childhood help us deal with emotional turmoil. For example, a child who learns to fly under the radar in an abusive home in order not to bring attention to himself may end up suffering less abuse over the course of time. However, when that child brings the same coping mechanism into his adult world, he faces a new set of problems – including people labeling him as unapproachable or socially awkward.

"Unhealthy coping mechanisms developed in childhood help us deal with emotional turmoil."

This can lead to more feelings of rejection, insecurity, and abandonment, making the garbage bag heavier and bulkier. Worse yet, in many cases, he represses the abusive memories and ultimately cannot understand why he acts the way he does. He believes it is his personality and nature.

In other situations, adults not only clearly recall the abuse they suffered, but they also spend a great deal of time reliving it over and over in their heads. Writing in the *Journal of Biblical Counseling*, Robert D. Jones, pastor of the Grace Fellowship Church in Hurricane, WV, referred to this as "bad memory flow."

Bad memory flow is when negative events from the past play like a loop in your head, haunting you time and time again. Traumatic events we think we put behind us long ago continue to pop in our minds unexpectedly, causing us anxiety and regret. What's happening?

The brain is attempting to take these negative events and create a scenario in which the victim is empowered. However, due to the intensity of the emotional pain the victim experienced, he or she doesn't have the ability to create a reasonable perspective or understanding of what happened.

Thus, the haunting trauma plays again and again. These memories lead victims to seek distractions from the anxiety and stress by acting out through unhealthy behaviors. Worse yet, these troubling thoughts continue churning and working to keep the victim in a perpetual state of victimhood.

A troubled childhood can have major ramifications for adults. H. Norman Wright, a renowned Christian therapist and author, points out that we may be attracted to people who are similar to those who hurt us in the past:

"Our attraction and attachment to people in adulthood can be a carryover from our past. If our parents were loving, we are more likely to be drawn to secure and good people. If they were cold and neglectful, we would tend to be drawn to those types of individuals as adults."

"A woman with a distant father will choose to date men like him who will turn out to be undependable, but she will see it as an opportunity to help him," says Wright. "A son raised by a mother who is aloof and unloving, will more likely date women who are emotionally distance. He keeps trying to refashion women to make them give him what he needs. An only child who did not have much experience relating to his peer group is more likely to select a parent figure for a spouse."

What we are doing in these circumstances is subconsciously trying to recreate the situation we endured as children, but this time we believe we have the skill set to manage the situation and make things the way they should have been.

Unfortunately, this approach rarely works since we are attempting to get other individuals to change to meet our needs. This is one of the reasons why some people move from one abusive relationship to another. They don't realize that what they are trying to do is to recreate their lost childhood, but this time to "get it right" and live happily ever after.

God and Our Garbage Carrying

At the onset of trauma in our lives, the challenge of living the abundant life God wants for us is placed in jeopardy. The weight of our garbage bag negatively burdens us as we move from season to season. Instead of experiencing clean starts and looking ahead with optimism, we instead are weighed down and believe little joy awaits us in our new ventures.

We may become bitter and resentful. We may even blame God, wondering why He has not given us an escape from the emotional pain we've carried for so long. On the other hand, some of us develop the belief life will never be rewarding or fulfilling and there is no sense in complaining. We check out.

In both circumstances, God is saddened. We tend to forget God knows what it feels like to experience loss, to suffer. He shed tears seeing His Son tortured and nailed to the cross. God knows what it is like to endure emotional distress. This is not a foreign concept to Him.

And because He understands the pain that comes with trauma, what do you think it does to Him when He sees one of His children suffer at the hands of another individual? I believe it makes Him sad and angry. God understands our suffering and He has compassion for us. He asks that we gather our pain and bring it to Him. He requests that we put our trust in Him to help us view our trauma in a different light.

"Those who suffer He delivers in their suffering; He speaks to them in their affliction." (Job 36:15, NIV)

"Humble yourselves, therefore, under God's mighty hand, that he may lift you up in due time. Cast all your anxiety on him because he cares for you." (1 Peter 5:6-7)

Do you know the story of Joni Eareckson Tada? Nearly 50 years ago, as an active and athletic teenager, she became a quadriplegic when she dove into shallow water. After dealing with her initial grief, what did Joni do with the rest of her life? Well, she launched the Joni and Friends ministry, which for more than 35 years has delivered resources and encouragement to those with disabilities.

Her Christian ministry assists people throughout the world and has been a source of inspiration and hope for thousands. Joni refused to sit and live her life carrying a bag of garbage; instead she turned to God and asked Him to show her what she should do with her pain. He, in turn, told her to use her testimony to help others who have suffered similar tragedies. She became a popular speaker, author, and artist. Joni is a wonderful example of what God can do with our pain.

God can and will help us deal with our trauma if we are brave enough to bring it to Him. *"And we know that in all things God works for the good of those who love him, who have been called according to his purpose"* (Roman 8:28, NIV).

Carrying garbage from the past serves no good purpose. It only serves to keep you weighted down as a victim. It's time to drop the garbage bag – the shame label – and place it at the feet of Christ. It's time to move on with life.

Your Roadmap to Thinking, Feeling and Acting Differently

- **Reflecting Upon Your Past**
- **Removing Your Shame Label**
- **Put Accountability Where It Belongs**
- **Understand How God Sees You**
- **Using Your Testimony**

1. Reflecting Upon Your Past

It is sad some of us experienced severe emotional, physical, verbal and/or sexual trauma in our lifetime. But the way we currently think, feel and behave does not need to be influenced and held captive to our previous hurts. We can put the pain in its proper place and begin the process of living the abundant life God intended for us.

But for this to occur, we need to do some heavy lifting. Work is required to sort out painful memories. Nearly every time I bring up the idea of exploring a painful past with clients, they balk, saying they don't see a need to go back and deal with the trauma.

What they fail to understand is the strong correlation between their past trauma and their current patterns of negative thoughts, emotions, and behaviors. That is why I am a big believer in what I call "connecting the dots" to help uncover those correlations.

"Connecting the dots of our past traumas helps us understand why we engage in negative behavior."

Connecting the dots helps us understand why we engage in negative behavior. By understanding why we think, feel, and do the things we do, we have a better chance of making real progress.

Psychologist and author Albert Ellis, says it is never the events themselves that distress us; instead it is our perceptions of the events. In many cases, our self-perceptions are incorrect, which in turn can lead to self-loathing and shame.

By understanding how our perceptions are formed, (usually as the result of direct and indirect messages received from others as we were growing up) we can challenge our misperceptions to determine their truthfulness and validity.

A troubled past influences our behaviors of today more than we can imagine. Growing up, we were not only influenced by people and events – they also hard-wired us. Hurtful people and painful events added lasting bits of garbage into our bags. In many cases, we have done such a good job of burying those pains we do not even recognize that they impact us today . . . or why.

Determining the rationale for our negative behaviors can be difficult when it involves examining painful events of the past. But knowing why you think, feel and do the things you do can provide amazing insight and resolve for making positive changes. It's OK to be afraid to look into the garbage bag, but do not allow that fear to prevent you from exploring what is inside it.

So how do you begin processing past, pent-up trauma? Knowing the severity of the trauma and its negative effect on your current life should help you determine whether to attempt to process this on your own or to seek the help of a competent mental health professional. If you elect to try on your own, I recommend a book entitled *Making Peace with Your Past* by H. Norman Wright. It is filled with exercises to gently help you walk through the process. However, if you start working alone, be sure you have a safety valve to draw upon to give yourself much-needed breaks. That safety valve can be a trusted friend, support group, pastor, or even hobby that can re-energize you after completing a work session. And if you find the process to be more difficult than you thought, please find a Christian counselor who specializes in treating trauma.

2. Removing Your Shame Label

Stirring up memories of the past can also stir up the shame that has been instilled in us. Shame is the most toxic and destructive of all emotions and can prevent us from moving on with our lives. If we do not remove our shame label, it will continue to paralyze us and negatively impact all aspects of our lives.

As John Bradshaw writes in *The Shame That Binds You*: *"Finally, when shame has been completely internalized, nothing about you is okay. You feel flawed and inferior; you have the sense of being a failure. There is no way you can share your inner self because you are an object of contempt to yourself. When you are contemptible to yourself, you are no longer you."*

One of the most effective means of overcoming shame is to talk about it. By telling our painful stories repeatedly, we lessen the negative impact they have on us. In turn, we become desensitized to them. Soon, we find they no longer have a death grip on us; instead, we control them.

One way to tell your story is to write a letter to those who abused or neglected you. The letter never needs to be sent or read to the person responsible for the shaming. In my practice, less than 10 percent of the clients who participate in this exercise send their letter. *Letter writing is for the benefit of the victim.* It is an extremely effective outlet for expressing painful thoughts and emotions that have been neglected for years.

Journaling is also a healthy way to work through the shame of our past. In the evening, spend 15-30 minutes outlining some of the negative thoughts and emotions you encountered throughout the day – along with what you believe may have triggered the thoughts and feelings. There is something therapeutic about journaling that helps quiet highly emotional thinking and moves you to more rational and responsive cognitive thinking. You'll discover the process of journaling reduces those racing negative thoughts. Also, going back and rereading what you've written helps you process the thoughts to determine if they are rational or irrational.

We also want to develop what I call "pillars". Pillars are the supporting elements of our self-esteem and provide us with a foundation we can turn to justify our worth. Pillars consist of key attributes about our personality and character. For example, in creating pillars, you may point out the following traits about yourself: *honest, smart, dependable, flexible, devoted, and modest.* And you'll want to add accomplishments such as: *graduated from college, raising three children, caregiver to ailing father before his death, blog writer.*

Once you've completed your pillars, place it somewhere so you can review it every day. Note this is a living document and you can add to it as new pillars are formed. If you are struggling to come up with a list, reach out to friends and family asking them to provide insight on how they perceive your strengths.

Finally, as we will discuss more in-depth in a moment, looking toward God for assistance (getting His point of view) is invaluable in dealing with shame. One of the insidious problems with shame is that shame-filled people are afraid to turn to God out of fear of rejection. A young woman I counseled who had been battling drug addiction for years told me, "How can God love someone as disgusting as me? I have sold my body to strangers just so I can get high. He can't possibly love me". She could not be more wrong in her assessment of how God sees her. In describing herself as "disgusting", she was talking about how she sees herself – but she incorrectly believes it is the way God sees her.

"Fear not, for you will not be ashamed; be not confounded, for you will not be disgraced; for you will forget the shame of your youth, and the reproach of your widowhood you will remember no more. For your Maker is your husband, the Lord of hosts is his name" (Isaiah 54:4-5, ESV).

Like that young woman, we believe God is ashamed of us because we project on Him how we feel about ourselves. God is our Father, and He chose us; we did not choose Him. He desires a close, intimate relationship with us and wants us to experience an abundant life. It is not His desire to heap more condemnation on our shame, but to help us break free of it.

"One of the insidious problems with shame is shame-filled people are afraid to turn to God out of fear of rejection."

"And straightening up, Jesus said to her, 'Woman, where are they? Did no one condemn you?' And she said, 'No one, Lord.' And Jesus said, 'Neither do I condemn you; go your way. From now on sin no more'" (John 8:10-11, NAS).

3. Put Accountability Where It Belongs

One of the saddest parts of dealing with trauma victims is watching them struggle as they attempt to take blame for what occurred. This happens due to the shame that often accompanies trauma. Shame leads trauma victims to believe they are bad people. It is not uncommon to hear a trauma victim take the blame upon themselves for the hideous actions of others.

Linda had been sexually abused by a neighbor for three years starting when she was 8. The abuse occurred almost daily as Linda came home to an empty house after school. The only child of a single mother, Linda was told by her mother to allow the neighbor to stop by and check on her every day. She never told anyone of the abuse because of the threats the man made to her.

Later, as a teenager, Linda was raped on two occasions by different men. And as an adult, she endured several incidents of sexual harassment in her workplace. In therapy, it was not uncommon for Linda to take responsibility for the crimes of these men. *"Perhaps I wanted him to touch me,"* she would say about the elderly man who abused her daily. *"If I did not want it to happen, I would have done something to stop it.*

*"Even with the second man who raped me, the dress I was wearing that day was far too short. I was a walking billboard that screamed **** me. I am such a pig!"* Linda was extremely tough on herself during our sessions, often referring to herself in extremely vulgar terms. Her shame led her to believe

she had wanted the abuse she had endured because she was a bad woman.

However, as we explored what had occurred, Linda came to understand that her "incident memories" were not accurate reflections of the actual attacks. Instead, they were her re-interpretation of the assaults. It is through these re-interpretations that she created erroneous thoughts and perceptions regarding the circumstances, which led her to place blame on herself instead of on the men who raped her.

That is what shame labels do. They cause the victim to believe she is a bad person. This, in turn, leads to the individual attempting to justify her role in the abuse, and how she may have encouraged or "wanted" it to happen. It is an attempt to reinforce the misconceived notion that she is indeed bad.

Cases like Linda's demonstrate the need to hold accountable the people who hurt us so shame labels can be removed. By holding people accountable, we come to see the reality of the trauma and remove any mistruths we have developed including self-blame. Honest accountability allows us to look back and objectively determine the facts of what occurred and to stop blaming ourselves for the sins of others. It allows us to begin the process of clearing our conscience and processing our shame.

Holding those responsible also helps us start to work on forgiveness, which frees us from developing bitterness and resentment. Forgiveness is not easy; nor is it always a "one and done" process. We may believe we have forgiven, but later realize we are still filled with anger towards the person or people who pained us. That requires us to go back and revisit the pain, (grieving) so that we can once again forgive and move on.

One of the most effective ways to learn to forgive is to develop empathy towards those who hurt us. Dietrich Bonhoeffer once said, "*We must learn to regard people less in the light of what they do or omit to do, and more in the light of what they suffered.*"

Bonhoeffer was speaking of those individuals who did not give us what we needed as children (safety, security, affirmation, attention) or who gave us what we didn't need (abuse or neglect). In either circumstance, when we can start to look at these individuals with different eyes (the eyes and heart of Christ) and understand the reasons behind their actions, (their brokenness) we can start to develop empathy for them, which in turn will help free us to forgive them.

4. Understand How God Sees You

When processing emotional and physical pain from the past, it is important that we understand how God sees us. So many people who wear a shame label believe God has cast them away or looks at them with disappointment. But that is not our God.

He sees you and me as His children and understands the pain and suffering we have experienced. God calls us to come out of the darkness and stand in the light where He stands. He tells us not to be afraid to show Him our shame because He already knows our shame. What He wants is to help us remove it. No child of God should suffer from shame. Drop to your knees and tell God why you feel shame. Call upon Him to remove the shame label and cleanse your soul with His love and acceptance. Begin walking the path of experiencing a new you and a renewed life – a path of spiritual freedom.

"God tells us not to be afraid to show Him our shame because He already knows our shame. What He wants is to help us remove it."

When you pursue God, you learn to see yourself as God sees you. You draw closer to Him by engaging in honest prayer, reading His Word, joining in Bible studies and small groups with other believers. You embrace God when you make it a priority to change your heart and make Him the focal point of your being. That means putting everything else behind Him – spouse, children, career, hobbies, passions, and pleasures. It also means being vulnerable and allowing yourself to confess your sins and weaknesses with Him. It is allowing Him to nurture you and show you the intensity of the love He has for you. He wants to do just that – let Him!

"For the Lord God will help me; therefore, shall I not be confounded: therefore have I set my face like a flint, and I know that I shall not be ashamed" (Isaiah 50:7, NIV).

5. Using Your Testimony

Joni Eareckson Tada took her tragic accident and turned it into a testimony that has made positive changes in the lives of thousands of disabled individuals. Our testimonies are powerful tools that not only shape and strengthen the Kingdom of God but also allow us to heal.

Imagine for a moment your shame label has been torn off and you are no longer crippled by shame. Now imagine encountering someone who is wearing a shame label similar to what you once wore. What if you had the chance to provide that person with inspiration and guidance on how he, too, could remove his shame label? How would that make you feel? Probably like an individual who has a purpose. That is what our testimonies provides us – a sense of purpose that we can make a difference in the lives of others who are struggling.

Your testimony allows others to see how God has taken a difficult event in your life and gave it value. It provides inspiration and hope. How do you create a testimony? Start writing your story. Simply write it without editing or stopping to make changes. Once you are finished, put it aside for a couple of days and then come back and start the editing process. The break also will provide you with an opportunity to think of elements you may have missed the first time around.

Once you have your testimony completed, share it with a safe friend or family member. We do this not to get input from the listener, (although that may be welcomed) but to practice telling our story. Then it's a matter of keeping your eyes and ears open to see what opportunities God provides you to share your testimony. Believe me—opportunities will come!

No matter what has happened to us in the past, there is always an opportunity to learn something about ourselves from the trauma we faced. We no longer need to carry our garbage or use unhealthy coping mechanisms to help us deal with our pain. Instead, we can move forward and finish well.

CHAPTER 4: THE SHAME OF STAYING STUCK

"You are not stuck where you are unless you decide to be."

–Wayne W. Dyer

I don't know about you, but I struggle at times trying to get things right. It is not as though I'm a blatant sinner who intentionally sets out to do wrong or cause harm. I am more of an "unconscious" sinner who messes up because I don't take the time to stop and think how the consequences of my actions will impact myself and those around me.

We all experience this type of sin. The negative thought that pops into our head about someone we are angry with. The scorn remark we allow our tongue to make before our brain can compute the pain it will inflict. The lustful glance we struggle to break away from when an attractive individual catches our eye. The lack of patience we experience when standing in the check-out line behind the person who can't figure out how to work the self-pay checkout counter.

We all engage in sin. Some are deemed as minor, while others are major offenses. But the problem isn't that we sin. There is no getting around our sinful nature. The real problem is when we repeat the same sin over and over. We don't learn from our mistakes, and we find ourselves stuck in the same recycling pattern (see illustration). When we are stuck, this behavior pattern develops a sense of frustration and feeling of shame that comes upon us because of our inability to break this destructive cycle. In this cycle, we may believe we are not in control of our actions. We struggle and white-knuckle ourselves through another day to stay sin-free. It is a constant battle and it feels as though we are forever losing. Our battle cry is "can I hold this off for one more day?" The answer is usually – no.

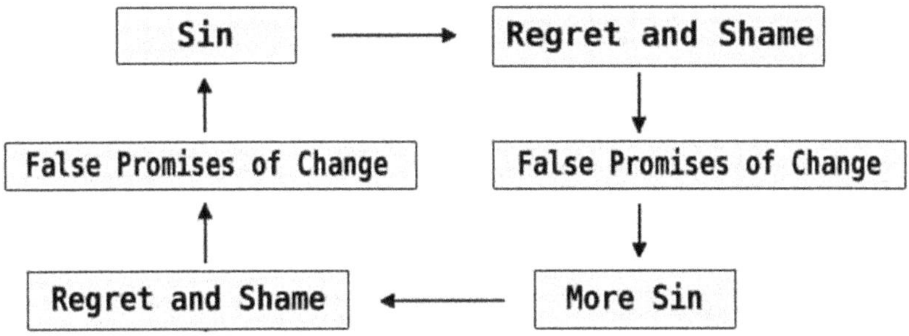

Bob is a husband and father. Bob also is undependable. He has made a habit of not being able to keep commitments or promises. Time and time again, he tells people one thing and does another. His wife and children believe he is selfish, and his employers feel he is unreliable.

This behavior caused Bob to lose multiple jobs as well as endure the wrath of his disappointed family. Although it is never Bob's intent to frustrate and disappoint others by not following through on his commitments, he continually finds himself trapped in the cycle where he ultimately does the wrong thing. So why can't Bob get this right? Isn't it as simple as being less selfish? Unfortunately, it is not that simple.

Bob's behavior is the result of a habit he developed as a young child to protect himself. He grew up in a home with a very demanding mother, who never allowed him to have a voice or pursue his desires. To keep the peace, he learned to tell her what she wanted to hear and went along with her demands. He learned at a young age that he could stop her excessive screaming and get her off his back by saying yes.

But this behavior resulted in Bob developing into a passive individual who rarely said no to anyone's request. He also rarely fulfilled their requests. Why? Because whenever Bob would comply with the wishes of others, it would stir up subconscious feelings of resentment – emotions like those he felt as a child. Those emotions were linked to a young boy who was angry for needing to give in to the constant demands of his controlling mother. As a child and teenager, Bob learned to follow through with his mother's demands to avoid conflict and her anger. But now as an adult, Bob possessed an internal anger that manifested itself in passive-aggressive behavior.

He wanted to avoid conflict at all cost due to his fearful nature. So Bob gave people answers he thought they would like to hear. However, due to his suppressed anger, Bob rarely followed through on his commitments. This resulted in facing the same conflict he was initially seeking to avoid by saying "yes" to every demand.

After professional help, Bob could see the frustration he caused others. But still he struggled to change his behavior because he refused to deal with his underlining fears or admit his hidden anger. He wanted to change but he was frightened to face the pain and hurt of the past. He basically did not want to "hear his mother scream any more" even if it was only in his mind.

Bob was allowing his fear to prevent him from "getting it right" and learning to live a more peaceful and fear-free life. He elected to just try harder. However, he would continue to cause frustration with family, friends, and employers, while enduring the shame due to the cycle of bad behavior he could not break.

But what does "getting it right" mean? Do we need to be perfect in all of our actions? Must we carefully map out everything we say or do to ensure it will be well received? The fact of the matter is you and I will never get it right all the time on our own. Even God knows this and so He supplies the Spiritual Helper:

"...for all have sinned and fall short of the glory of God and all are justified freely by his grace through the redemption that came by Christ Jesus." (Rom. 3:23-24)

Every day, I see people who are seeking meaningful and permanent changes in their troubled lives. In many cases, these individuals believe they are incapable of changing since they have tried and failed numerous times in the past. They feel stuck. But real change is not achieved by "white knuckling" and hoping for the best. It requires allowing your heart to be transformed. And that takes courage, and sometimes requires touching painful nerves to determine how things went so terribly wrong. How did we get hardwired to the point where our thoughts, emotions, and/or behaviors are out of control?

But some people like Bob don't want to investigate the source of their problems – therefore they remain stuck.

But stuck is not how God wants us living our lives. The Christian life is about movement. When we are stuck and not moving toward God, we can experience many emotional drains such as:

- A lack of joy because we are existing and not living
- A decrease in energy because we are bored and unmotivated
- An increase in our shame as we feel helpless in our struggle against our poor behaviors
- A sense of dryness in our relationships
- A belief that God is not with us

A lack of movement in our lives brings with it feelings of hopelessness and despair. It is as though we are sitting in the dark waiting for someone to shine a light, so we can see where to go. We find this place extremely troubling because we are not designed by God to be stuck. Being stagnant is contradictory to the Christian life. We are created to always be moving forward – being transformed – even if we are taking baby steps.

"But real change is not achieved by "white knuckling" and hoping for the best. It requires changing your heart."

The Christian life is like a running stream that is pure, cool, and refreshing. It is forever moving, allowing the rocks in its path to help keep it clear and fresh. And as it moves, it spills over onto the banks bringing life to things around it.

When we are stuck, we are like a puddle of water. That puddle sits still and eventually will become dirty and toxic. Over time, it will dry up.

As Christians, if we elect to be puddles of water our growth in Christ will be nonexistent. We will feel isolated, alone and eventually, we will shrivel up and quit. However, if we manage our life like a continuously moving stream, we will find God playing an active role in all aspects of our lives. This is the path of sanctification, and when we stay on it – even in times when we feel like getting off – we will continue being transformed into Christ's image.

But as I said before, moving from stuck to active can be very difficult and frightening. Generating real change in our lives can't happen if we rely only upon ourselves to implement it. We need a higher authority. But again, this is where many struggle because in their shame they believe God is disappointed and doesn't love them. Accordingly, they say "God doesn't hear me and has no interest in helping me". But they are wrong.

You see, God loves sinners. Moses was a murderer; David committed adultery; Noah had a drinking problem; Paul had anger issues and Rahab was a prostitute. God did not hate any of these individuals. In fact, God used them to demonstrate His glory. God doesn't hate sinners. God hates the "sin" but He doesn't turn away from us because of our sinful ways. It is through our relationship with Jesus Christ who serves as our intercessor that we are accepted by the Father.

*"Who then is the one who condemns believers? No one. Christ Jesus who died – more than that, who was raised to life – is at the right hand of God and is also interceding for us" (*Rom. 8:34).

If anyone would be tearing us down and pointing out our sins to God, it would be Satan.

Jesus is not condemning us for our sins. Instead, He is telling the Father "they are mine". If anyone would be tearing us down and pointing out our sins to God, it would be Satan. But Jesus will have no part in that. Through the Holy Spirit, He is ready to offer guidance, transformation, and support if we do one simple thing. Turn to Him. He is not judging us but instead, He is there to help us repair our broken souls and walk with us along the path as we attempt to learn to abide and walk in faith.

Although He serves as our intercessor, we Christians should not fall back into believing we are too weak to follow Jesus' teachings. If we blatantly sin claiming temptation is too strong, we are liars.

"No temptation has overtaken you except what is common to mankind. And God is faithful; he will not let you be tempted beyond what you can bear. But when you are tempted, he will also provide a way out so that you can endure it." (1 Cor. 10:13)

Yes, I do believe there are times when we need God's supernatural intervention to help us, especially when it comes to forgiveness. But to say the temptations we face in life are too strong for us to manage is wrong and disputed in the Scripture above. God doesn't want us to fail because He realizes in many cases not adhering to His command will leave us filled with shame. He did not create us to be shameful beings but instead, to experience a life in which we find our identity in being His children.

When we blatantly sin, we are dishonoring our Lord Jesus Christ and what He did by going to the cross for us. While this does not mean our salvation is in jeopardy, it is a direct sign of disobedience and unbelief in our Lord's promise. "*...You are not your own; you were bought at price. Therefore, honor God with your body*" (1 Cor. 6:19-20). If we blatantly sin, where is our remorse? Where is our shame? Where is our appreciation for God's enormous sacrifice of His Son?

In their book, *"Every Man's Battle"* Stephen Arterburn and Fred Stoeker encourage Christians to use the verse above as a shield to protect ourselves against sinful temptations. As they point out, "*we do not have the authority" to fulfill all selfish desires wherever and whenever we want*".

You and I "do not have the authority" to act out as selfish children, who just want what we want. Instead, we need to grow up and understand living the Christian life is about Spiritual Maturity, which requires sacrificing our control and allowing God to take control.

Clients who struggle with sexual integrity issues sometimes hit a wall in therapy and find themselves acting out occasionally. This can cause great distress because they feel as though they are forever failing. At this point, I lead them to the verse above, as well as 1 Cor. 13:11, "*When I was a child, I talked like a child, I thought like a child, I reasoned like a child. When I became a man, I put the ways of childhood behind me.*"

These two verses have helped some of my clients understand that taking a white-knuckle approach to change doesn't work. Instead, they should look to honor Jesus Christ for the sacrifice He made for them on the Cross. They should seek Him with all their thoughts, emotions, and behaviors. For the closer the relationship we have with our Lord and Savior, the less likely we are to intentionally act in destructive ways. But this can only happen when we are moving forward in our walk with God.

It is a miserable feeling being stuck and not growing in our relationship with God. When this occurs, we can assume that either our passion for God has been side-tracked or never fully existed. We find ourselves experiencing a void in our souls, as we look around and see fellow Christian brothers and sisters on-fire for the Lord and exhibiting their joy in feeling God's presence in their lives. But what allows one individual to experience the intimacy of God, while another individual – with good intentions – can't generate those same feelings? The person who is wrapped up in God keeps moving. That is the difference between a Spirit that is on fire and a Spirit that is burning out.

When I was in my re-birth phase and learning all I could know about God, I thought I was so pumped up with energy and excitement. The inside of my head looked like God TV 24-hours a day. It was all I could think about. But as time went on, I realized that while I had indeed generated a great wealth of knowledge about God and Christianity, it was all in my head. You see, little had penetrated my heart. It was as though I had draped myself with a veil of Christianity for the entire world to see, but if they could examine my heart, they would have discovered nothing was very different.

"The person who is wrapped up in God keeps moving. That is the difference between a Spirit that is on fire and a Spirit that is burning out."

It was only after attending a Georgia Presbyterian Pilgrimage weekend – a Christian retreat – that my heart began to melt and open. It was there I experienced the enormous outpour of love from complete strangers, who were giving up their time and money for one reason – to help people like me to establish a meaningful relationship with Jesus Christ. And it worked. All the passion for God that was in my head began to shift to my heart, and I started the process of surrendering my life to Him. After nearly 40 years, I was finally moving.

The God Answer to Moving Forward

What does that movement look like? In a word – love. Loving God more. Loving others more. And loving ourselves less. The more we allow ourselves to love and be loved, the further we will move in our walk that leads us closer to God. It is also a shame remover. When we are focused on giving and receiving love, there is no place for shame. It can't exist with love.

Movement also is about the on-going change that occurs in a person's thinking, attitude and behaviors. The reality of this transforming change is seen as our focus shifts from "inward" to "outward". We find ourselves more concerned with others and how we can make a difference in their lives. Our selfishness begins to fade.

Pastor and author Dallas Willard talks about this "fading of our selfishness" and how it impacts the worldly values that lead to our sinful actions, *"Can I still think about such things?" you may ask. Yes, you can. But you increasingly won't. And when you do, as formation in Christ-likeness progresses, they won't matter. In fact, they will seem ridiculous and uninteresting."*

"The more we connect with our Spiritual self, the uglier sin looks."

The more we connect with our Spiritual self the uglier sin looks. However, it is critical to remember that in your transformation, while sin may not have a stranglehold on you, it's never fully eliminated. For you see, no matter how committed we are to live in the Spirit we are still housed in these sin-ridden bodies. And that leaves the door open for us to slip back into old destructive behaviors. Therefore, we need to always be on alert to temptations and triggers that weaken our resolve to continue our spiritual journey and keep us marching forward.

"Be alert and of sober mind. Your enemy the devil prowls around like a roaring lion looking for someone to devour" (1 Peter 5:8).

When we are on track and moving in the right direction with our Christian growth, we think less of this world and more of the world to come. We realize our ills – no matter how burdensome – are temporary and will be gone on the day of our last breath. The wonderful Christian band, MercyMe, has a song entitled "In the Blink of an Eye" which is what this life amounts to in time. It's gone in a flash. But instead of making our objective "getting" the most out of it, we should be focused on "putting" the most into it.

During our time here, if we devote every ounce of ourselves in an endless effort of loving and being loved, we can hopefully expect to one day hear the words "well done good and faithful servant".

Movement comes back to two words – Christian Maturity.

But what does Christian Maturity look like? Well, as Christians we are called upon to undergo God's continuous transformation in our lives leading us away from worldly values and moving our focus toward Spiritual values. This is accomplished by allowing the Spirit to lead and saying "no" to things we would like to do but are hurtful for us and others around us. We need to learn to say "no" when tempted with an extra donut; "no" to sexual lust; "no" to making nasty remarks to the person ahead of us who can't figure out how to work the ATM; "no" to self-centered behaviors.

Paul in Romans 12:2 wrote, "*And do not be conformed to this world, but be transformed by the renewing of your mind, that you may prove what the will of God is, that which is good and acceptable and perfect.*"

This process is a never-ending journey in which we commit ourselves to be obedient to the Lordship of God's Spirit and His Word. This is not an easy process, especially considering the constant messages we are exposed to regarding worldly living. Messages such as:

- Living together before marriage is a good way to determine if you're right for each other
- If you don't look out for yourself, no one will
- Get as much as you can from life because it is too short
- Your self-worth comes from how others view you
- If you are not attractive, you will struggle in this world
- Never forget, never forgive
- You deserve to be happy always
- The one with the most toys wins
- If you want it done right, do it yourself

These are messages that if we follow, will lead us down a path of despair and frustration. If we yield to their on-going temptations, we will seek "stimulation" in order to feel positive about ourselves.

In her book, *Fundamentals of Christian Education*, Ellen White says this about the impact of worldly values *"The continual craving for pleasurable amusements reveals the deep longings of the soul. But those who drink at this fountain of worldly pleasure will find their soul-thirst still unsatisfied. They are deceived; they mistake mirth for happiness; and when the excitement ceases, many sink into the depths of despondency and despair. O what madness, what folly, to forsake the "Fountain of living waters" for the "broken cisterns" of worldly pleasure!"*

Change is possible when we approach it from the right direction. Let's explore some steps for helping us get unstuck and keeping shame at bay.

Your Roadmap to Thinking, Feeling and Acting Differently

- **Reviewing Your Spiritual Map**
- **Repent**
- **Understanding the Past**
- **Managing Negative Thinking**
- **Moving Away From Worldly Values**
- **Understanding the Concept of Imperfect Progress**

1. Determining Where You Stand

You can't start moving unless you know what direction you need to move in. To help you determine the proper course, conduct a Spiritual checkup to see where you currently stand in your walk with God. Take time, at least three or four times a year to ask yourself hard questions like these and note your answers:

- ☐ Am I growing in my faith? What evidence do I have to demonstrate my answer?
- ☐ Do I feel my relationship with God is deeper today than three months ago? If no, why not? If yes, in what ways?
- ☐ Am I spending enough time studying God's Word?
- ☐ What condition is my prayer life in? Why?
- ☐ Do I fear becoming closer to God? Why?
- ☐ What false idols do I desire more than God?
- ☐ Am I making an effort to put the needs of others before me?

- When have I put my family and others ahead of myself? When have I not?
- Am I harboring resentment against anyone? Who and why?
- What sin(s) have I kept hidden away from others? What am I doing to rid myself of them?
- Have I been allowing God to guide my actions for His Glory? If not, why?
- Have I been honoring and appreciating Christ's love and the sacrifice He made for me?
- Do I allow myself to be vulnerable, to share my emotions and troubles with others? If not, why?
- Why do I feel a sense of shame?

With the Lord leading, put together an action plan to strengthen those areas you perceive as weak. Focus your efforts on solidifying your relationship with God. Do not approach this exercise as a series of tasks, but invite God to begin softening your heart and showing you how to live in His love.

2. Repent

A key to getting unstuck and removing our shame is knowing and believing we are forgiven of our transgressions. It is interesting to see how many Christians struggle in believing God has forgiven their sinfulness. But it is true.

"For he has rescued us from the dominion of darkness[1] *and brought us into the kingdom*[2] *of the Son he loves,*[3] *in whom we have redemption, the forgiveness of sins."* (Col. 1:13-14).

This includes all our sins – past, present, and future. They have been wiped away through the performance of Jesus Christ on the Cross. We have but one task to complete – repent when we engage in our sinful nature.

"If we confess our sins, he is faithful and just and will forgive us our sins and purify us from all unrighteousness" (1 John 1:9).

Let's start by examining the true nature of repentance, which goes beyond asking for the forgiveness of our sins. Repentance is a commitment to move away from our sinful nature and to adopt behaviors and attitudes that are pleasing to God.

It is not simple. It will feel uncomfortable moving away from sinful behaviors, but learning to embrace and tolerate the discomfort allows us to move into the reality of feeling God's love and presence. Overtime the level of discomfort will lessen. Done right this becomes an opportunity to transform our failures into opportunities for real and positive character changes that will lead to healthy Spiritual growth.

If on the other hand, we elect not to repent of our sins, we will find ourselves back once again in the same sin-regret-shame cycle outlined earlier. We must understand that to make sincere efforts to move away from our sinful habits, we need to make a conscious effort to continually grow Spiritually and allow change in our hearts. And that takes courage.

Christian author John Maxwell says this about Spiritual growth, *"If we are growing we are always outside our comfort zone"*. How true. Although it is not impossible, it is more difficult to grow Spiritually when things are going well in our lives. It is during the storms that we have the opportunity to demonstrate our faith and trust in God, and with that comes the reality of Spiritual growth. That is not to say we can't grow during prosperous times, but to Maxwell's point, we probably need to move out of our comfort zone to begin to grow.

The problem? Who likes being out of their comfort zone?

3. Understanding the Past

It is difficult to break the sin cycle and cleanse ourselves of shame when we don't understand why we act in destructive ways. As we discussed in Chapter 3, if we understand the reasons behind our negative thinking, feelings and actions, we have a strong advantage and better opportunity to make the positive and life-long changes that we desire. But sometimes that requires understanding our past to comprehend what troubles us in the present. Many of us were negatively impacted by trauma and neglect by both internal and external influences during our childhood and youth.

Go back and "connect the dots" to see if past wounds play a role in your faulty thinking today. But remember, uncovering trauma and neglect from our past can be a very emotional process and should be done with the help of a competent mental health professional. Keeping the pains of our past shoved aside can limit our ability to make real change in our lives. It can limit us in giving and receiving emotional intimacy and can negatively impact the way we feel about God. Real change can happen when we are honest with ourselves and we confront the fear regarding the pain that lies deep within us. However, we must identify what we are dragging around before we can throw it aside.

4. Managing Negative Thinking

We are more likely to remain stuck when we are living in a cesspool of negative thinking. The secret to managing negative and racing thoughts is awareness. We must become more self-aware (cognitive) of our negative thinking early in the thought process before it spirals out of control. This is a critical step and requires discipline and practice. Here is an example.

A client I had been working with for sexual addiction was making progress but continued to suffer from intrusive sexual thoughts that would lead him to masturbate. After journaling each time he had this urge, we noticed a pattern – which is not unusual for individuals facing his dilemma. We could identify he was prone to encountering a higher volume of sexual thoughts during times when he was experiencing low levels of stimulation.

I refer this to being "drained". Low levels of stimulation could result from being: tired, hungry, lonely, bored, angry, depressed, etc. To battle against low stimulation, our mind begins to move us toward thoughts, ideas, and fantasies that increase our level of excitement by raising levels of dopamine and serotonin to the brain. These are pleasure enhancing chemicals that have been demonstrated to be similar to receiving a shot of morphine. Basically, we are getting high. Here are some serious and unhealthy stimuli:

- Drugs
- Alcohol
- Promiscuous sex
- Pornography
- Excessive television viewing

- Internet surfing
- Uncontrolled shopping sprees
- Excessive food
- Living for work
- Endless video game playing

You get the point. If we are not careful and engage in unhealthy, high-stimulating behaviors often we can find ourselves facing an "addiction". This pattern begins with negative thoughts that are left unchecked, which in turn results in highly-charged emotional thinking. Unlike cognitive thinking, which is more rational in nature, emotionally-charged thinking is often impulsive and can lead to poor decision-making and behaviors.

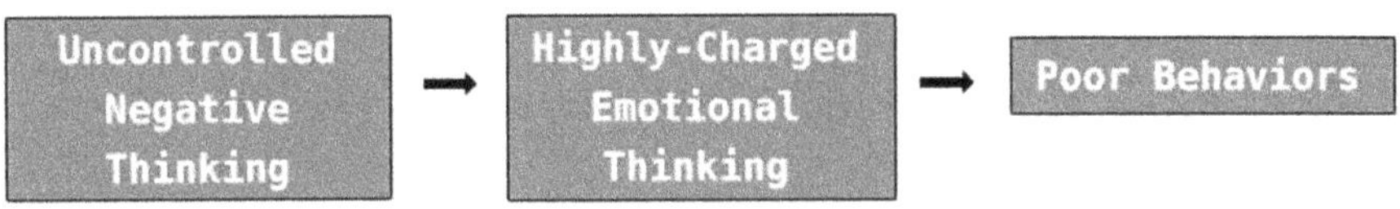

We can short-circuit this destructive process by learning to take control of our negative thoughts. Now you may be saying "I don't think that is possible." But it is. All of us are capable of controlling how we think. For example, suppose you're driving, and your car starts to hesitate. Your initial thought may be "Oh no, I wonder what is wrong". That is a reasonable thought. But it's what we do with our thought process following the initial thought that determines our ultimate emotional state. If you follow-up the original thought with, "I will stop by the mechanic and have him check it out" you will probably remain concerned, but your anxiety level will remain in check.

However, if you follow-up the original thought with a line of thinking such as the following, you may find yourself in a complete state of panic and frustration.

"Oh no, I wonder what is wrong?"

"I can't believe this car is going to give me problems now."

"I bet it needs a tune-up."

"That is going to cost me a fortune!"

"I can't afford to pay for a tune up. I just received the bill for Billy's orthodontist work and that is already setting me back this month."

"And how in the world am I going to pay for that new tennis club membership that my wife just signed up for?"

"She is so irresponsible. She should never have done that without asking me."

"I am so tired of her constantly overspending. What is wrong with her that she is so selfish?"

"She doesn't give a damn about anyone else but herself. I hate when she gets that way."

"I'm going to call her right now and let her know the mess she put us in!"

"What starts out as a simple thought can turn into an overwhelming concept if we "feed" the thought with more negative thinking."

I thought he was concerned with his car? How did his wife become the major point of frustration? Because he would not stop "feeding" his negative thoughts. He allowed his thoughts to run amuck and his emotional state spiraled out of control.

Has this ever happened to you? Probably more times than you would like to admit. We need to understand what starts out as a simple thought can turn into an overwhelming concept if we "feed" the thought with more negative thinking.

Here is another example. Let's say a thought enters your head about your spouse who is running late for a party you're going to attend. "I can't believe she is going to be late again." Basically, that is an innocent thought, and it could cause you some distress because you don't want to be late. However, let's take that same thought and feed it with more destructive thoughts.

"She ALWAYS does this."

"I think she does this on purpose."

"She is just trying to make me look bad in front of my friends."

"She never liked my friends anyway."

"She is simply stalling."

"She wants me to be angry, so she has an excuse not to make love with me tonight."

Sex? How did his wife running late lead him to think about sex? The women reading this are probably answering – because he's a man. Anyway, back to our subject at hand.

Of course, the examples I have provided are slightly exaggerated. But can you see how one negative thought can turn into a raging war within your mind? And it happens to all of us every day, throughout the day. So, what is the answer to calming negative thinking?

We can begin by being more cognitive of our negative thoughts. We need to become aware when our minds start to wander with impure, hateful, self-defeating, or angry thoughts. Once we are aware of what we are thinking, we should tell ourselves "it is just a thought" and make no attempt to feed it with additional thoughts.

Then we can evaluate the circumstances we are facing and determine how they may be influencing our thinking. In the example above, the husband was getting angry, which would have a negative effect on his ability to be cognitive of his thought process. Ultimately, he would need to take steps to reduce his highly-emotional state, so that he could rationalize the situation. Having done that he would see that he could either accept his wife's chronic tardiness or inform her he would meet her at the event the next time she is running late.

A sexual-addicted client of mine started having strong sexual thoughts while studying in the college library. He was totally taken aback by the experience and could not understand why such thoughts would enter his mind in that setting. When we looked deeper, we found out that he was completely bored by the assignment he was working on – which involved studying Shakespeare. The great playwright was draining my client, which led to the development of intrusive thoughts. I wonder how many other people have a similar problem with Shakespeare?

There are many circumstances that drain us including: boredom, loneliness, stress, feeling hungry, being angry, sickness, restlessness, etc. However, just identifying what is draining us emotionally, mentally, physically or Spiritually is not enough. We must look to replenish ourselves with healthy stimulation, if not, we will most likely continue to act out in a negative fashion. This falls in line with the parable Jesus tells in Luke 11:24-26.

"When an impure spirit comes out of a person, it goes through various places seeking rest and does not find it. Then it says, 'I will return to the house I

left.' When it arrives, it finds the house swept clean and put in order. Then it goes and takes seven other spirits more wicked than itself, and they go in and live there. And the final condition of that person is worse than the first."

We cannot simply push the intrusive thought aside and go back to what we were doing. If we do, it will return with vengeance and take on a greater power than it had originally. Instead, we must address the low stimulation we are facing and seek healthy ways to replenish ourselves. I call these lifelines.

What are healthy lifelines? Well, that depends on the individual. Here are some examples how to replenish yourself:

Listening or playing music
Praying and reading Scripture
Going for a walk or run
Playing with children or pets
Watching a comedy
Reading
Spending time with a friend
Taking a relaxing bath
Exercising

Spend time creating a list of healthy things that can increase your stimulation level, therefore providing you with a strategy to put in place the next time intrusive thoughts hit. Remember, be cognitive of your negative thinking and be aware of the circumstances that may be draining you.

5. Moving Away From Worldly Values

For many Christians, being stuck is the result of being focused on worldly values and buying into the promises of worldly living. The flesh is weak. You have heard that numerous times. But it is true. Therefore, we must build a strong emotional attachment with the Holy Spirit by continuously putting aside worldly distractions from our minds and allowing ourselves to focus on the positive events surrounding us at the moment. This allows us to respond to all situations with the power of the Holy Spirit, rather than succumbing to our natural reactive tendencies, which are driven by our sinful nature.

"Do not conform to the pattern of this world, but be transformed by the renewing of your mind. Then you will be able to test and approve what God's will is – His good, pleasing and perfect will." (Rom. 12:2)

Do you know what I love about this verse? It's the payoff. In this payoff we find one of God's greatest promises in which we will be able to discern "His good, pleasing and perfect will." What a wonderful promise! And to receive it, we need to allow Him to turn us away from worldly values. Oh, that sounds easy enough! Uh, no it doesn't.

In fact, it is difficult to turn away from the allure of worldly values. The mindset of "but I want to do that" is hard to break. Because – let's face it – we enjoy many of the sinful pleasures we engage in. Did I say that?!! But it is true. If we did not enjoy acting upon sinful ways, they would not be such a struggle to break. We would simply ignore them. Satan would be out of business. But that is not the case –unfortunately, there is often fun found in sin.

Add to that the values and temptations the world attempts to sell us every day through media and advertising. With a "do whatever pleases you" banner shoved in our faces continuously, it becomes very tempting even for Christians to succumb to the dark side. That is one of the reasons why I believe it is difficult to be a Christian. We are called upon to be different and not allow ourselves to conform to the world's standards. This takes not only conviction and determination but also a level of humility to understand that we can't fight our sinful nature alone. Instead, we must rely on God's power to assist us.

"We can't fight our sinful nature alone but instead we must rely on God to assist us."

As shut out worldly values when we:

- ☐ Filter and tune out ungodly and impure images and materials from our homes and offices
- ☐ Monitor what we allow our eyes to see and our ears to hear
- ☐ Decide to lead our families, by demonstrating a strong moral fabric
- ☐ We engulf ourselves routinely in the Spirit and Word of God

Being a Christian is hard. And it is not uncommon for people outside the Christian community to look at us waiting to see us fail. And we do! That is because we are human. But if we continue to monitor ourselves to ensure we are not being drained (mentally, emotionally, physically and/or spiritually) and we continually engage in self-reflection, we can stay on the right path and trip less. But when we fall, we get up, brush ourselves off, and ponder "what have I learned" so we can continue to move forward in our walk with God.

6. Understanding the Concept of Imperfect Progress

An important point to understand when implementing real change to our long-rooted negative thinking, feelings and behaviors is that change is a process. During this process, we are going to experience success and failure. We are going to experience wins and losses.

This is what I term *"imperfect progress"*. While we are attempting to get it right always, we may suffer temporary setbacks. Yet, we continue to move forward after each slip and do not allow it to deter us from achieving our final goal of being transformed.

Once people understand this idea of imperfect progress it allows them to make a misstep without beating themselves up too hard. Instead of failing, becoming discouraged and quitting on the change process, they allow themselves to experience God's mercy. This is also helpful for spouses who are walking with a partner who is struggling in a particular area of sin such as an addiction. This imperfect process allows them to demonstrate empathy to their loved one knowing they are trying to change, but also understanding it is a process and not a one-and-done effort.

The bottom line to change is this – when we allow Christ's love to penetrate and truly become part of us, we open ourselves to experiencing real change. We come to understand we are not *commanded* to be more loving, joyful, gentler and kinder but instead, we are *compelled* to do so. We are on the path of being transformed to become Christ-like. And in doing so, God will take our hardened hearts and soften them. We will experience a renewing change not like that of the chameleon but like the butterfly.

"I have been crucified with Christ and I no longer live, but Christ lives in

me. The life I now live in the body, I live by faith in the Son of God, who loved me and gave himself for me." (Gal. 2:20)

Getting it right all the time may not be easy for us but it is for God. By conducting on-going self-reflection; being cognitive of our negative thinking; understanding why we do the things we do; staying replenished; moving away from worldly values; and allowing the Holy Spirit to become a reality in our lives, we will increase our odds dramatically.

"Trust in the Lord with all your heart and lean not on your own understanding; in all your ways acknowledge him, and he will make your paths straight." (Proverbs 3:5-6)

CHAPTER 5: THE SHAME IN BEING DISTRACTED BY DISTRACTIONS

"The truth is, of course, that what one regards as interruptions are precisely one's life." –C.S. Lewis

Karol runs like the speed of light, and she doesn't even own a pair of sneakers. For a single mother of two teenage boys and with a successful dental practice, there is no time for slowing down. As we sat in my office and discussed the concept of her finding some down time to relax I could see her anxiety grow.

She came to see me because she was having trouble sleeping, feeling lonely after having been divorced for five years, and issues with her teenagers. As we talked, I saw "living fast" had been Karol's MO for her entire life. Growing up in a home with an abusive father, she found numerous activities to get involved with in order to be out of the home as much as possible. She described herself as a "driven" student who was frustrated with any grade lower than an "A". In college, she put her "nose in the books" and graduated near the top of her class. Karol was always putting lots of time, energy, and effort into everything she did and she is now exhausted. She attributed her behavior to what she called a "driven nature" but what she was doing was running away from her emotional pain.

Her marriage ended in part because her husband, also a dentist, complained she was never available for him. Instead, she was much too invested in their dental practice. He ended up having an affair and leaving her for another woman.

Even after her marriage ended, Karol could not slow down. You see, she utilized a defense mechanism of a busy schedule – that she created as a child – to avoid time with her abusive father. And while that defense mechanism served her well as a child and teenager, it was causing havoc in her life as an adult. Running non-stop had become a way of life for her because it was all she had ever known. Her defense mechanism, which she should have stopped using when she left home, was no longer working for her and causing undue stress and anxiety.

There are many people like Karol who can't slow down. They are always in a rush and always on the move. But busyness can go far beyond simply causing exhaustion; it also can be destructive for relationships as Karol saw with her two sons. She was so involved in her work and maintaining her home that she was not making time for her children. Even when all three of them were together, Karol's mind was on work or her chore list. Her busyness was creating a wedge between her and her sons, which was leading to their rebelling against her.

"People-pleasers feel they must be performing acts of service to others to gain acceptance. That requires a lot of work, effort and energy."

While Karol stays busy to avoid sitting still and running the risking of dealing with her emotional pain, others live life fast because they are people pleasers. People pleasers have a difficult time saying no or setting limits. They often believe it is what they "do" and not who they "are" that keeps people liking them. Their mindset is, if they work harder and longer than others, they will be accepted and appreciated. The problem with this approach, however, is these individuals are forever worrying about their performance slipping and therefore, disappointing people who ultimately will abandon them.

In her book, "*You're Not Crazy – You're Codependent*", Jeanette Elisabeth Menter points out *"people pleasers are created by the emotional abuse or neglect they suffered in the form of withholding love and affection. They lack confidence in their ability to maintain strong relationships with others based on who they are as individuals. Instead, they feel they must constantly be performing acts of service to others to gain acceptance. That requires a lot of work, effort, and energy. It is a lifestyle that eventually leads to resentment and burnout"*.

But even if you are not a people pleaser, you may find yourself so busy you don't remember what day of the week it is or where yesterday went. And it may not be the result of a busy schedule. Many people are living fast because they can't get their minds to slow down. They are imprisoned by their continuous rambling and racing thoughts that distract them from their surroundings.

Although it is problematic that we allow ourselves to be so distracted due to our busyness or racing thoughts, what is more troubling is we are missing out on numerous opportunities to engage with others and enjoy a fulfilling life. I am sure many of you would agree that it is possible to be in the same room with someone but mentally be miles away. Now, doing this occasionally is normal, but when you're constantly stuck in your own head you have the making of a serious problem.

The God Answer For Slowing Down

Being stuck in your own head not only cheats you out of intimate interactions with others but it also impacts your relationship with God. The Christian life encourages us to turn to God for guidance when it comes to discerning decisions such as employment, relationships, finances, etc. That requires an ability to spend time in solitude and silence so that we can begin to clearly hear God's voice.

"Being stuck in your own head not only cheats you of intimate interactions with others, it also impacts your relationship with God."

"My sheep follow me because they know my voice... my sheep listen to my voice; I know them, and they follow me." (John 10:27)

Talking and listening to God are two of the most important directives of the Christian life. It is by and through His Spirit and Word we are given the direction and guidance we need to be faithful servants. But for many Christians, there is so little time in the day that something must give.

Unfortunately, in many cases that is the deepening of their relationship with God.

Another result of an overly busy mind is we are so preoccupied with negative issues or our to-do list that we miss the numerous blessings that surround us. Have you ever wondered "where are God's blessings in my life" or "why have I not received more blessings"? The answer may be God has provided blessings, but you have been too busy to notice them. And of course, there is this question – "have we taken the time to ask God for guidance and blessings"?

As Christians, we are called upon to see where God is at work around us. That is quite a difficult task to accomplish when we are trapped inside our own head and adhering to our own schedule. Do you think potential opportunities to make a difference in another's life may have passed you by because you were too busy? Unfortunately, this probably happens more often than we would like to admit.

When we are distracted, we not only miss out on establishing genuine relationships and fulfilling activities, but we also suffer the greatest loss of all – we take our eyes off the desires of God's heart. We see this with the Apostle Peter when a great wind erupts as Jesus walks across the lake to meet with His disciples. Peter initially has trust in Jesus and gets out of the boat to walk towards Him until…

"But when he saw the wind, he was afraid and beginning to sink, cried out, "Lord, save me!" (Matt. 14:30)

What happened? Peter became distracted when he took his eyes off Jesus, which nearly led him to drown. During those times when we feel we are drowning due to demanding work schedules, family issues, financial crisis, illnesses, do we have our eyes on Christ? Or are we trapped in our own heads ruminating over and over about our problems?

The way you answer those questions will determine if you will have peace and tranquility in your life or sadness and chaos.

Your Roadmap to Thinking, Feeling and Acting Differently

- **Determining Your Priorities**
- **Getting Out the Cutting Shears**

- **Slowing Everything Down**
- **Learning to Be Mindful**

1. Determining Your Priorities

At some point, all of us feel overwhelmed as we experience the feeling that life is getting out of control. One moment things are going smoothly and the next we are surrounded by chaos. That is simply part of living. But for those individuals who find themselves racing in circles and always feeling like they are running behind, the issue may be their priorities are out of balance. Jesus' directive on priorities were very clear as outlined in Matthews 6:33. *"But seek first His kingdom and His righteousness; and all these things shall be added to you"*.

Chip Ingram is the senior pastor at Venture Christian Church in Los Gatos, CA and leads a ministry called Living on the Edge. In this small group study entitled, *Balancing Life's Demands,* he outlines what he believes is the optimal approach Christians should take in determining priorities. They are:

- God
- Spouse
- Children
- Work
- Ministry

According to Ingram, having the right priorities allows us to live life without becoming overwhelmed. Balance is everything in life. Too much of anything is never good for us. This also applies to the priorities we set in life. Too much work leads to poor relationships. Too much commitment to our children leads to a drifting apart between husband and wife. Too much emphasis on ministry work could result in poor financial issues.

A couple with seven children ranging in ages 2 to 15 came to see me because of marital issues. The husband, who managed a restaurant, worked approximately 70 hours a week. Not only was the relationship between him and his wife in need of repair, but he complained his children did not respect him. In speaking with the older teenagers, I came to learn they felt they did not need their father and saw him as being unavailable. In their eyes, his work was his priority and because of it, his most important relationships were failing.

Ingram points out the priority order of God, spouse, children, work, and ministry leads to a healthy lifestyle. He also acknowledges our priorities must shift and adjust depending on circumstances. When the boss drops a major project on your desk with a tight deadline, more emphasis needs to shift to your work. A child becoming seriously ill becomes our number one priority. The key to managing priorities is being able to move back to the optimal priority order - God, spouse, children, work, and ministry when our crisis is over.

Individuals who experience the sinful desire of distracted living are living out-of-control. They lack the ability to establish priorities because they can't get out of their own head and control their racing thoughts. In their mind, there is always something to do, which keeps them from escaping the "Cycle of Shame".

"His (God) is the most reliable route to follow when life gets complicated."
-Chuck Swindoll

Establishing priorities is critical to helping us live a less complex life. If these individuals do not slow down, they open themselves to major stress issues that could lead not only to relational difficulties but physical problems. In working with clients who live life too fast, many cannot grasp the concept of priorities. "*You don't understand. I do not have a choice. These are things that need to be done and I am the only one that can make it happen.*" I can understand that type of thinking. In fact, back in the days when I was working in the corporate world and focusing on worldly values, I often used the same excuse. But that is all it was - an excuse.

Once again, read the words of Chuck Swindoll regarding the benefit of putting our priorities in order. "*You want joy? You really want what is best? Simply consider yourself having different priorities than your associates and seek*

God's way. His is the most reliable path to follow when life gets complicated. It will have its tough moments, but you will never regret it."

God is and always should be the focal point of our lives. When we can accomplish this, we will discover our way of life will change dramatically for the better.

2. Getting Out the Cutting Shears

There comes a time in life when we may feel so overwhelmed that we need to evaluate our situation and determine what changes are required to get us back in balance. Part of that process may be shearing back something(s) from our lives in order to reduce our anxiety level and make things more manageable.

We can utilize cutting shears for removing destructive relationships; a dead-end job; or to cut back on what seems to be an endless list of activities and chores. In as much as we would like to remove destructive things from our lives, sometimes it is not possible to do it with one swift cut, but instead, it requires time to remove all the debris.

For example, let's say your job is extremely stressful, with long hours and endless travel that takes you away from your family. The people you report to demand you make the job the number one priority in your life. You miss spending time with your family and the job has become a source of discontentment for you and your wife. Your boss has little empathy for your situation and says the job "is what it is". You can go elsewhere but similar companies will offer similar problems. Add on top of that your current lifestyle requires a certain amount of income. What can you do?

You start praying about generating a plan that includes shearing the job over time. But what are your options? Perhaps you can look to go back to school and pursue another line of work that you are interested in but doesn't have such a demanding workload. Perhaps you can look to downsize your lifestyle, so you will be able to take a different job that may pay less but offer a slower pace. Those are examples of potential options.

The point is shearing can come in handy when we are faced with situations and people that are making our lives sad and difficult.

3. Slowing Everything Down

"The Lord is my portion," says my soul, "therefore I will hope in him." The Lord is good to those who wait for him, to the soul who seeks Him. It is good that one should wait quietly for the salvation of the Lord." (Lamentations 3:24-26)

It can be difficult to be still, especially in this age of super technology. If we are not busy with what life is throwing at us, we are trying to distract ourselves with our smart phones, tablets, computers, etc. We can't stand being still! But to lead an abundant life and reduce stress, we need to learn to slow everything down.

The French philosopher Blaise Pascal is quoted as saying, *"All men's miseries derive from not being able to sit in a quiet room alone"*. Well said.

Because both sinful and healthy desires are based heavily on our thoughts and emotions, we should develop the habit of praying and challenging all desires to determine their true merit and intent. If we slow everything down and process our thoughts and emotions with the light of truth, love, and logic before reacting, we will experience better behavioral outcomes. If we can control our thoughts and emotions long enough to determine if they align with the Fruit of the Spirit, we will find ourselves making better decisions.

But how? Again, it takes some prayer, planning, and discipline.

- ☐ Blocking your work calendar for 15 minutes both in the morning and afternoon so you can collect your thoughts
- ☐ Learning to say no in order not to overextend yourself
- ☐ Shut off the smart phones, tablets, and other devices to give yourself a break
- ☐ Turn off the radio and drive in silence
- ☐ Practice limiting your response time. There is no need to reply immediately to every text and email. Practice holding off on immediate responses
- ☐ The same holds true to personal interactions. There is no need to say the first thing that comes to mind. Practice the art of processing and

discerning what others are saying before providing your own response

Being still and learning to slow everything down also provides us with the ability to open and recalibrate our hearts, so we can clearly see the direction God has for us. How can we hear God if we take no time to listen?

4. Learning to be Mindful

How many times have you said to yourself "I have no idea where the time went"? Probably more often than you would like to admit. Most of us have a bad habit of being so caught up in our own heads (thoughts) we can't be present in the moment. That is where being mindful comes in.

Being able to re-train yourself to slow everything down and live in the moment will go a long way in reducing your anxiety level. In very simple terms, being mindful is being aware of your surroundings and what you are currently doing. This is not easy and takes a great deal of practice. But the benefit of being able to be aware of what is going in the moment can lead you to make more rational decisions and appreciate what is happening around you.

For example, when you find yourself stuck in the house over the weekend to finish a work assignment, take several breaks to go outside and appreciate nature; engage in a conversation with your spouse or children; or involve yourself in a conversation with God. Understand there is more going on around you than the work assignment.

Dr. Linda Mintle explains to Christians that mindfulness is an active process between God and us. *"God is mindful of us and we are to put on the mind of Christ. To do so, we meditate on who God is and listen to Him in prayer. Daily, we renew our minds by the power of the Holy Spirit working in us, love God with all our mind and implant God's laws into our minds. Meditation is a way to connect with God, to cling to God, to listen for His voice and allow Him to align our hearts with His."*

Our sinful desire of living too fast can have devastating impacts on our health, relationships and overall way of living. But when we make time daily – throughout the day – for God, we can learn to relax despite our current circumstances.

"Rejoice in the Lord always. I will say it again: Rejoice! Let your gentleness be evident to all. The Lord is near. Do not be anxious about anything, but in every situation, by prayer and petition, with thanksgiving, present your requests to God. And the peace of God, which transcends all understanding, will guard your hearts and your minds in Christ Jesus. Finally, brothers and sisters, whatever is true, whatever is noble, whatever is right, whatever is pure, whatever is lovely, whatever is admirable—if anything is excellent or praiseworthy—think about such things. Whatever you have learned or received or heard from me, or seen in me—put it into practice. And the God of peace will be with you." (Phil. 4:4-9)

Oh, in case you missed it – read the last line of that verse again. And again. And again.

CHAPTER 6: THE SHAME OF CONTAMINATED THOUGHTS

"Would you feel unashamed if someone could read your thoughts? Well, God can." – Eddie Capparucci

Jill described her childhood environment as "trailer trash". Growing up in a poor, rural community, she had a severe speech impediment, which led people to believe she was not very intelligent. She was put into special education classes and was frequently told how stupid she was by her mother and other children. Jill's father died when she was four-years-old and her mother, a high-school dropout, worked menial jobs to make ends meet. As a very young child, Jill was often left alone for hours as her mother worked. Television became her only friend.

At age 7, her mom remarried, and things went from bad to worse for Jill. Her stepfather was an abusive man both verbally and physically. He refused to allow her to make friends and go outside and play. Meanwhile, her uncle repeatedly sexually abused her over a period of seven years. At age 16 she left home and went from the frying pan into the fire. Jill married a man who was a drug addict, even more abusive than her stepfather.

Over the years, the verbal and physical abuse was constant, and Jill learned to walk on egg shells. She only spoke when spoken to. In her head, she would degrade and belittle herself following the example of others who had done the same to her. She was filled with contaminated thoughts that resulted in creating a shamed-filled individual.

Her husband was demanding in the way their trailer was kept and would conduct inspections when he returned from work. From the moment she woke up until she went to bed, Jill would search the trailer finding something to clean or straighten just to ensure everything was to her husband's satisfaction. But she was searching for the impossible. There was also his demand for sex whenever he asked, which was every day and often several times per day.

After 14 years of marriage, her husband died in a car accident. After his death, she went through a long period of grieving and missing him. You see, although he was abusive, she saw him as one of the few people who ever accepted her. She confused his abuse for love. In reality, he was using and manipulating her but she never recognized that due to her contaminated thinking and shame.

Although the abuse had stopped her negative thoughts and shame remained. She saw herself as defective and not deserving of happiness. To quiet the negative self-talk, she began to drink heavily and over the next five years became a full-blown alcoholic. Her relationship with God was non-existent due to her shame, which told her God thought she was dirty and unworthy of His love and attention.

"We believe these shame-inducing thoughts as truth and not only think of ourselves in a negative manner, but act out in harmful ways that reinforces these thoughts."

Having gone through detox and recovery, she came to see me complaining of extreme anxiety and poor sleep habits. Although she had not had a drink in nine months, she complained she could never slow down. From the moment she woke up heading off to work until her late evening AA meetings, she made a conscious effort to keep herself busy. And when she would get home around 9 p.m., she would clean her apartment until two or three in the morning. There was no such thing as "mellowing out" in Jill's world.

Why was Jill this way? Because when she was occupied with activities, it slowed down the destructive, negative thoughts that haunted her. The fear of sitting still and allowing the contaminated thoughts to creep into her head caused her anxiety to rise, thus, leaving her fearful of relapsing.

Jill's negative self-talk painted the picture of a woman who suffered from extreme low self-worth. Based on input from various people who abused her,

Jill saw herself as: lazy, ugly, stupid, promiscuous, fat, worthless, clumsy, and trashy. And all of this left her loaded with shame. In many cases, our self-talk is developed via criticism received from external sources in our lives, especially when we were a child and teenager. Over time, we come to believe these shame-inducing comments that were thrown at us and accepted them as truth. In turn, this resulted in low self-worth that escalates the negative opinions we have about ourselves.

I can recall the story of a female client whose father not only was hyper-critical of her throughout her childhood and teen years, but also started questioning her moral standards if she missed her curfew even by only a few minutes.

She recalled one of his reactions during one of our sessions. *"I was 15 and I got home 10 minutes late. I had been out with several of my girlfriends. He was standing at the door waiting for me and I could see his face was red. He didn't ask any questions but just started shouting at me. He called me a whore and slut. He said my makeup made my face look like a clown, even though I was only wearing a light shade of lipstick. He said my skirt was too short, although it sat just above my knees. He told me that I could not live under his roof if I was going to act like a slut. Then I looked at the top of my stairs and there stood my mother doing nothing to defend me. She just stood there. So, I assumed she felt the same way.*

"After that night, everything in the house changed; outbursts and name calling became the norm," she continued. *"After a while, I thought what the hell, if he thinks I am a slut I may as well become one. And I did."*

This young girl got "cornered" into her father's demented, fearful, and hateful world. She was far too young to be able to process what he was telling her was the result of his own distorted view of women. He was dumping "his stuff" on his daughter – his own fears and prejudices, his biases, and his view of women. He dumped it on her and she allowed it to stick. This man ended up shaming his daughter and she ended up paying the price for it.

In her popular book, *"Men Who Hate Women and The Women Who Love Them"* Susan Forward says, *"We all tend to believe criticism more than we believe praise. One cruel statement can have much more impact than 20 positive ones."*

That teenage girl allowed her father's hurtful comments and her mother's passive behavior to define who she would become as an adult. Once she gave them the power to do that, she lost. She took the shame they inflicted and magnified it numerous times with her promiscuous behavior. And the more she engaged in shameful behaviors, the louder her negative self-talk became. And worst yet, she thought God agreed with her parents and wanted nothing to do with her.

But even if we have not endured traumatic events such as the ones mentioned above, all of us have dealt with people and events that have shaped how we see ourselves. Family, friends, and others have inflicted us with shame-inducing words and actions, even if not intentionally. But whether purposely or not, their words stick, and they play repeatedly in our heads, leaving us to believe they represent a realistic view of who we are as individuals. Far too often, we allow the hurtful words of others to define us. One of the keys to handling contaminated thoughts and controlling our shame is to better understand how this type of thinking can gain a stronghold on us.

Well-known psychologist Albert Ellis came up with an interesting and helpful method for aiding us in better understanding our dysfunctional thinking. Entitled, "Rational Emotive Behavior Therapy" (REBT), this approach is an action-oriented psychotherapy that teaches individuals to identify, challenge, and replace their self-defeating thoughts and beliefs with healthier thoughts that promote emotional well-being.

"Far too often, we allow the hurtful words of others to define us."

Part of this approach includes what Ellis referred to as the "ABCs" of dysfunctional thinking. "A" is the activating event; "B" is our belief of the event; and "C" is the consequence of the event. Ellis theorized that it is not "A" or even "C" that causes irrational thinking but instead, "B" our beliefs of the event. Look at some of these examples of A-B-C thinking.

- My girlfriend broke up with me (A) and I felt very alone and rejected (C). I am not loveable and will be alone for the rest of my life (B).
- My boss did not include me in the meeting today (A) and I am very

confused why he would do such a thing (C). I bet it means I am probably on my way out of this company. I will probably get fired any day now (B).

- My teenage son is ignoring me (A) and I feel pretty offended (C). I must be an awful parent for him to treat me that way. What is wrong with me? (B)

Our perceptions and beliefs about circumstances, people, and events in our lives can lead to an endless flow of irrational beliefs that can result in poor emotional responses and intensified shame. While we can't control all "activating events" that take place in our lives, we do have control over our beliefs about those events.

"We allow one negative thought to spiral out-of-control and create a world wind of hateful self-talk in our heads."

Where most of us get into trouble is when we are not cognitive of our thought process. Therefore, our negative thinking escalates to a point where we engage in poor emotional responses and behaviors. Simply put – we allow one negative thought to spiral out of control and create a whirlwind of hateful self-talk.

Here is another example of irrational thinking that impacted me. My wife and I put together a marriage-training program that we offered at our church. The activating event (A) was that no one signed up for the course. The consequence (C) was that we did not do the course at the church. What was my belief (B) about the situation? I believed people in the church were rejecting me and questioning my knowledge and expertise to assist them in strengthening their marriages.

My irrational thinking led me into a week-long funk, in which I was feeling sorry for myself. However, I started to reflect on what my wife and our church pastor both had told me about conducting such a class. They believed most people would feel uncomfortable taking a marriage course at their own church in fear others may think their marriage was in trouble. I had ignored their thinking and moved forward with the idea, later having to learn the hard way what they said was true. Rethinking the situation, I concluded that no one rejected me. What they did was reject the idea taking a marriage class at their own church.

It is important to note sometimes the contaminated thoughts you experience may have nothing to do with the current circumstances you are experiencing. Instead, consider them the result of subconscious emotions that relate to past events or people that caused you emotional pain.

For example, let's say a good friend agrees to meet you for coffee but cancels at the last minute. You are deeply saddened, although the friend has a good excuse. The sadness leads to contaminated thoughts such as, *"I know she did not want to get together with me. It always happens that the people I try to get close to run away from me. It is obvious she has figured me out and sees how ugly I am inside. It was just a matter of time before she dumps me as a friend."*

You find your mood continues to sour and you start withdrawing from people justifying to yourself that "nobody really cares." However, what triggered your depressed mood – which you have failed to identify – is your friend canceling reminded you of what your father did to you time and time again as a child. He constantly would make promises to do things with you but would bail at the last moment.

While you should have every right to feel disappointed that the friend couldn't keep the date, it should not have taken you into an emotional tailspin. The reason you sunk to the emotional depth you did had more to do with the disappointment you still harbor for your father and his insensitive actions, rather than your friend not meeting you for coffee.

But our contaminated thoughts are not always focused on how we feel about ourselves. Our minds are loaded with negative thinking, whether it is how we perceive the world, our neighbor, politics, religion, or other ethnic races to name only a few. Our internal biases and prejudices that we work so hard to keep a lid on don't go away simply because we do not express them. We may try and kid ourselves that we are judgment-free when it comes to others but the thoughts inside our mind tell another story.

And that is the result of the darkness within our hearts. Because we are flesh, within each of us is a heart that contains impurities. At the core of that impurity is fear. It is fear that brings to life contaminated thoughts, which serve to expose what is in our heart.

"A good man brings good things out of the good stored up in his heart, and an evil man brings evil things out of the evil stored up in his heart. For the mouth speaks what the heart is full of." (Luke 6:45-49)

To the extent your heart remains darkened depends on how much effort you place in doing self-reflection about your weaknesses and the steps you take to overcome them. If you are smart and consistent about your approach to this exercise, your steps will lead you directly to God.

The God Answer to Our Contaminated Thoughts

In the quest to live an abundant life, it is critical we maintain a positive and upbeat attitude toward life. A key component to accomplishing this is keeping contaminated thoughts at bay. And how does God direct us to do that?

"Finally, brothers and sisters, whatever is true, whatever is noble, whatever is right, whatever is pure, whatever is lovely, whatever is admirable—if anything is excellent or praiseworthy—think about such things. "Whatever you have learned or received or heard from me, or seen in me—put it into practice. And the God of peace will be with you." (Phil. 4:8-9)

Did you notice the promise in the last sentence of that verse? If we focus on what is true, noble, right, pure, lovely, admirable, excellent, or praiseworthy, the peace of God will be in us. Sit with that for just a moment.

- ☐ Imagine saying goodbye to shame
- ☐ Shipping guilt away
- ☐ Erecting a shield to keep other's garbage off you
- ☐ Limiting your fears
- ☐ Experiencing true freedom!

This is what the promise can provide and all we need to do to experience it is to get God's help in changing our mindset. We need to learn to take every negative thought that enters our head and hold it captive as directed by the Apostle Paul.

"We demolish arguments and every pretension that sets itself up against the

knowledge of God, and we take captive every thought to make it obedient to Christ" (2 Cor. 10:5).

But notice, we are asked not only to take our contaminated thoughts captive but to also make them "obedient to Christ." What does that look like?

Well, it means looking inside our hearts to determine why hateful and dark thoughts about others would even enter our minds. It means examining our thoughts that focus on sinful behaviors, such as – lust, gluttony, envy, jealously, etc. – to determine why we would allow ourselves to entertain such destructive thinking.

All of this is a process in which we are attempting to move from a negative to a positive mindset. God is inviting us to accept a mission where we are allowing our minds to break free of the negativity that consumes and overpowers us.

Part of that mission is stopping the ridiculous practice of believing the stinking-thinking that tells you what an awful person you are. We need to stop believing the negative aspects of how we think about ourselves. Instead, we need to start believing what God thinks about us. And what does He think about us? He thinks we are precious.

"Who shall separate us from the love of Christ? Shall trouble or hardship or persecution or famine or nakedness or danger or sword? As it is written: "For your sake we face death all day long; we are considered as sheep to be slaughtered." No, in all these things we are more than conquerors through him who loved us. For I am convinced that neither death nor life, neither angels nor demons, neither the present nor the future, nor any powers, neither height nor depth, nor anything else in all creation, will be able to separate us from the love of God that is in Christ Jesus our Lord." (1 Peter 2:9)

"And what does He (God) think about us?
He thinks we're precious."

Others may condemn us. We may condemn us. But God does not condemn us. He accepts us in all our brokenness through the effort of Jesus Christ who died on the Cross for each one of us who believes. Your identity as the prince or princess of a King is defined only by God Himself and not by anyone who walks here on earth.

It is important to understand you have the power to ensure someone's words or actions cannot define who you are as a person. What it takes is:

- Becoming more aware of your own negative thinking
- Holding those thoughts up to God's truth about yourself
- Being able to re-frame contaminated thoughts into the positive attributes God recognizes in you

As we discussed earlier, at the heart of all contaminated thoughts are fear and shame. This fear and shame are materialized from the deep-rooted hurts of our past, such as the case with Jill. Once Jill was able to go back and analyze her irrational thoughts, she was able to see the damage others had done that resulted in her feeling shameful and consumed with contaminated thoughts. She then matched up those lies against the Voice of Truth – how God saw her and not how she saw herself.

There is no doubt she made some mistakes due to her faulty thinking. But as a child of God, she discovered she was unconditionally loved and accepted. There was no need for her to hide from Him any longer because of her shame – for He had removed it.

Your Roadmap to Thinking, Feeling and Acting Differently

- **Seeking to Identify Contaminated Thoughts or Moods**
- **Don't Feed Negative Thoughts**
- **Changing Your Mindset**
- **Feeding Your Soul**
- **Taking Them to God**

1. Seeking to Identify Contaminated Thoughts or Moods

This exercise goes back to the idea of being more cognitive of our thinking by staying mindful in the moment. The more we make an effort to be conscious of our negative thoughts, the better chance we have to limit the damage they can do. It also empowers us to determine how the thought originates and understand why it's irrational. Through this process, we can quickly change our mindset and move away from the contaminated thought.

However, many individuals have a difficult time staying in the moment and identifying their negative thinking before it gets out of hand. They struggle to realize the presence of their contaminated thoughts until the toxicity has been rambling in their heads for an extended period of time. The anxiety is already exasperated. For these individuals, I recommend becoming more aware of their mood changes. If one moment you are feeling fine and possess few worries and the next moment you are feeling saddened or angry, there is a good chance some negative thoughts are brewing in your mind.

Now, that is not always the case. For example, having lost my father at 5, whenever I see a scene in a movie where a father embraces his young boy, I get teary. There is no negative thought that enters my head, but instead, those scenes touch an emotional void that I experienced by this death. The feeling is one of being cheated out of a relationship with my father.

When we face irrational thinking it usually means we are also feeling depleted and drained. Perhaps we are tired, bored, lonely or anxious. Instead of allowing our irrational thinking to get the best of us, we should turn our thoughts to God and seek His intervention into our mindset.

"So, do not fear, for I am with you; do not be dismayed, for I am your God. I will strengthen you and help you; I will uphold you with my righteous right hand" (Isaiah 41:10).

The bottom line – be on the lookout early for contaminated thoughts.

2. Don't Feed Negative Thoughts

An important thing to remember about a contaminated thought is this – it is just a thought. If we leave the thought alone and turn our attention to more positive thoughts, it will most likely fade. But that is not an easy thing for us to do. Instead, we feed the initial negative thought with more negative thoughts.

This occurs when we aren't cognitive of the initial contaminated thought. Instead, we let it play out in our heads, feeding it more and more with negativity and creating a situation where we feel emotionally overwhelmed. For example, let's say your wife is late coming home from work and has not called. The initial thought may be: "I wonder where she is"?

Now watch what happens when this one innocent thought is left to wander freely.

I wonder where she is?

This is very unlike her to be this late.

And she didn't call. What is that about?

She always calls.

She is the most responsible person I know.

Oh my God!

Did something happen to her?

Let me call her cell again. No answer. Damn!

I know something is wrong!

I wonder if she had an accident.

I hope she didn't get hurt.

I couldn't bear that thought of losing her!

Oh Lord, what is going on? Please help me!!!

Conversations like that play in our mind on a regular basis. Maybe they are not as intense, but they play themselves out based on emotions and not facts. And those emotions are based on our feelings of fear or being offended.

All of us experience fear and worry in our lives. There is no escaping these two powerful emotions. However, it is when they become a constant in our daily living that we become too emotionally-based in our thinking instead of cognitive.

In his book, "*Could It Be This Simple*" Dr. Timothy Jennings, says this about emotionally-based thinking. "*When feelings are allowed to control the will, it will always lead to destruction. Reflect a moment on your life and consider your 10 most regrettable actions – what you wish you could undo or wish you'd never done. How many were based on feelings?*"

Not only do unchecked feelings such as anger, bitterness, selfishness and lust cause havoc in our lives, they also drive a wedge in our relationship with God. If we are allowing our feelings to lead us, then it goes without saying we are not turning to God and asking Him to direct our path.

We can help reduce emotionally-based thinking when we learn how to stop feeding our negative thoughts and focus instead on the logical aspects of our current circumstance. When a negative thought enters our mind, we must recognize it for what it is – just a thought. It contains no power unless we give it power. Take the example above, the thought that came to mind was "I wonder where she is?" That is nothing more than a thought. But what did we do with that thought? We fed it with additional negative thoughts snowballing it into the full panic mode.

Did something happen to her?

Let me call her cell again.

No answer. Damn!

I know something is wrong!

I wonder if she had an accident.

I hope she didn't get hurt.

I couldn't bear that thought of losing her!

This is a habit we all are guilty of from time to time. But there are some people who engage in this type of obsessive thinking on a regular basis. If we are to have less emotional turmoil in our lives, we must not allow our thinking to control us but instead realize with God's help, we can manage our negative thinking.

"Let your eyes look straight ahead; fix your gaze directly before you. Give careful thought to the paths for your feet and be steadfast in all your ways. Do not turn to the right or the left; keep your foot from evil." (Proverbs 4:25-27)

Take the time to allow God's wisdom to work within you and allow Him to remove the emotionally-charged scales that cover your eyes during times when you are feeling troubled or offended.

"Trust in the LORD with all your heart, and do not lean on your own understanding. In all your ways acknowledge him, and he will make straight your paths." (Proverbs 3: 5-6)

3. Changing Your Mindset

Once you have identified contaminated thoughts and stopped the process of feeding your negative self-talk, you can move to the process of changing your mindset. It is important to understand that it's not enough to simply block out a thought. This is called thought stopping and was a very popular technique at one time among therapists. But over the years, studies demonstrated thought stopping was not effective. It was discovered when a person tried to block out a thought, it would come roaring back a short time later with a greater vengeance.

Try this exercise. Put this book down for 2 minutes and sit quietly. But whatever you do, DO NOT think about purple rabbits. You can sit and think about anything, but I forbid you to think about purple rabbits. Go ahead and try it. I will wait for you to get back.

How did it go? Come on be honest. Didn't the thought of purple rabbit cross your mind once or twice? It is very difficult to say, "I simply refuse to think about that". It is like the parable of the unclean spirit that Jesus talks about in Matthew. When an impure spirit leaves a person, it wanders restlessly and then returns to the house in which it left and finds it clean but empty.

The same occurs with our mind if we do not replace our negative thinking with positive and pure thoughts. If we do not take this step, our negative thoughts will come back stronger and will cripple our ability to work through difficult times.

My wife and I had an opportunity to teach an adult Sunday school course called, "*The 4:8 Principle*" a book written by Tommy Newberry. The course and book are based on the scriptures from Philippians 4:8, which we examined earlier in this chapter. This verse is valuable in helping understand the importance of changing our negative mindset and focusing our thoughts on Godly thinking.

"We find peace when we seek it in the right places."

"Finally, brothers and sisters, whatever is true, whatever is noble, whatever is right, whatever is pure, whatever is lovely, whatever is admirable—if anything is excellent or praiseworthy—think about such things." (Phil. 4:8)

Another way to change your mindset is surrounding yourself with good and Godly people. John Ortberg is the senior pastor at Menlo Park Presbyterian Church in California, a leading author of numerous books. He says this about controlling his irrational thoughts: *"Never worry alone. When anxiety grabs my mind, it is self-perpetuating. Worrisome thoughts reproduce faster than rabbits, so one of the most powerful ways to stop the spiral of worry is to disclose my worry to a friend. The simple act of reassurance from another human being [becomes] a tool of the Spirit to cast out fear—because peace and fear are both contagious."*

We find peace when we seek it in the right places. We open our minds to be re-trained to help us escape sinful desires when we no longer model the behavior the world says is permissible. Instead, we ask Jesus to help us model our behavior after His.

"You were taught, with regard to your former way of life, to put off your old self, which is being corrupted by its deceitful desires; to be made new in the attitude of your mind." (Ephesians 4:22-23)

4. Feeding Your Soul

Another component in re-training your brain to focus on more positive aspects of life is monitoring what we are feeding our mind on a daily basis. Are we subjecting ourselves to music with demeaning lyrics; movies with nudity and violence; television that promotes "do whatever pleases you" behavior? Such a stream of unfiltered filth can have a devastating impact on the way we think and feel.

Author Wayne Dyer said, *"If we focus on what is ugly, we attract more ugliness into our thoughts, and then emotions, and ultimately into our lives."*

If this is what you have been subjected to, then perhaps it's time to change your mental diet. Maybe it's time to remove the constant exposure of unhealthy images and messages and replace them with a diet that consists of positive and uplifting materials.

What does this diet look like? How about things like Christian music, PG and PG-13 rated movies, books that provide inspiration, and television that is educational. Not to mention good and godly people to surround us and serve as a source of inspiration. Chip Ingram, pastor of the ministry, *Living on the Edge,* recommends conducting media blackouts on a regular basis to help slow down the steady flow of negative information we receive from major media outlets.

Now, let's face it, we can't lock ourselves away from all worldly messages. If we try, we would have little in the way of entertainment. But the key is moderation. I will admit I have been hooked on television programs that are not always PG. But overall, I monitor what I allow my eyes and ears to take in daily, and it can't be non-stop violence. Would I love to cut out all non-PG entertainment from my diet? Sure. But I am just not there yet. I have gotten a lot better over the years, but I still have a way to go when it comes to Christian maturity. The point is we need to continue to listen for and act upon God's Will every day. Even if we only take baby steps.

5. Taking Them to God

When controlling and contaminating thoughts enter your mind, you may find it difficult at times to manage them on your own. It is during these times we should bring these disturbing thoughts to God in prayer; asking for His assistance in turning these damaging thoughts and ideas into thoughts that bring Him glory.

When we train ourselves to bring unhealthy thinking to God, we will soon learn we have more discerning control over our thinking than we realize. For it is through the power of the Holy Spirit that we can overcome sins that haunt our lives.

*"Those who live according to the flesh have their minds set on what the flesh desires; but those who live in accordance with the Spirit have their minds set on what the Spirit desires. The mind governed by the flesh is death, but the mind governed by the Spirit is life and peace. The mind governed by the flesh is hostile to God; it does not submit to God's law, nor can it do so. Those who are in the realm of the flesh cannot please God. You, however, are not in the realm of the flesh but are in the realm of the Spirit, if indeed the Spirit of God lives in you. And if anyone does not have the Spirit of Christ, they do not belong to Christ. But if Christ is in you, then even though your body is subject to death because of sin, the Spirit gives life because of righteousness." (*Romans 8: 5-10)

CHAPTER 7: THE SHAME OF LOVING WITH CONDITIONS

"The test of love is that it gives, even when there is no expectation of a return."
–John Ortberg

Our worldview of what is right and wrong begins to take shape when we are children and teenagers. It is developed by influences that surround us especially parents, siblings, teachers, and friends. Sometimes one of the outcomes in the development of our worldviews is what I refer to as "demanding rules." These are self-imposed guidelines that were originally developed to help us determine if particular behaviors were right or wrong. Many of these rules can be very useful. However, when we expect everyone else to adopt these "demanding rules" they become shameful behaviors.

These adopted regulations are one example of the sinful desire that I call "Loving with Conditions". What do demanding rules of Loving with Conditions look like?

"I will love you always if you (fill in your own special requirements here)."

"If you really cared you would (fill in your emotional manipulation request here)."

Here is an example I witnessed with a couple who I assisted with counseling.

William hated being late. Wherever he needed to go, he made it a point to always be on time. It was a "demanding rule" he had been taught by his mother at a young age and one he chose never to question. "*You must NEVER be late. It is rude and inconsiderate to be late. Being late means, you do not care about others.*" That was the rule engrained in William's mind by his rigid mother.

Now being on time is a good virtue, but the reason it was a "demanding rule" for William was the anxiety he endured in remaining true to the rule. It was not enough for him to be on time for any appointment, instead, William had to be 10 minutes early in order not to feel emotional distress. If he needed to go somewhere for the first time, he would take a "trial" run the day before to ensure he would not get lost and be late.

Demanding rules occur when we take what began as a personal preference and push it to the extreme. Another problem with William's desire to be on time was he "demanded" the same punctuality from others. And when they did not meet his "demand" for being on time, he would become upset and annoyed.

However, his wife Brenda did not possess such a demand. In fact, she thought "rushing around gives people ulcers." Therefore, Brenda was rarely on time. This drove William crazy and resulted in serious dissension between the couple. William viewed Brenda's making him wait as a clear indication she did not care or respect him.

On the other hand, Brenda felt William was judging her as being self-centered by her chronic tardiness. More importantly, she felt William would withhold his love from her whenever she was late by withdrawing and sulking. *"Based on his behavior, I feel as though he stops loving me because I can't be on time,"* she said.

All of us have demanding rules we created over our lifetime. Here are examples of some:

- "Everything must always be in its place."
- "Being too emotional is a weakness."
- "Couples should do everything together."
- "Children should be seen not heard."

During couples' therapy, William revealed how his mother insisted he never be late. When he was not on time, she told him in no uncertain terms how disappointed she was in his insensitive behavior. She would then withdraw from William and give him the silent treatment for several hours or days. What mother was doing was shaming William. Therefore, in order to not expose himself to that shame, William demanded of himself to always be on time.

When Brenda heard this story for the first time, she felt sorry for William and became empathetic for his need to be on time. She started to work on becoming more punctual. At the same time, William began the work of processing the painful memories of feeling like a failure in the eyes of his mother. It was his hope that in time he could learn to ease off his demanding rule. He also went to work to show Brenda his love for her did not fluctuate based on her behavior. He wanted to demonstrate there were no strings attached to his love for her.

Some individuals withhold love because they become disappointed when they feel their desires and needs are not being met by their partner. This disappointment can be demonstrated in many ways including lashing out in anger, being passive-aggressive, or withdrawing. This behavior indirectly communicates the message "I don't love you right now". More importantly, it shames their partner.

"Some individuals withhold love because they become disappointed when they feel their desires and needs are not being met by their partner."

Take the guy who by most accounts is considered a good and decent husband but he just can't pick up after himself. He leaves a mess wherever he goes. His wife, on the other hand, can't stand the thought of having anything out of place. Over time she uses her frustration over his messiness and withholds sex. What is she indirectly communicating to him? "I will love you unconditionally and completely, BUT only if you start picking up after yourself."

Or the husband who badgers his wife about the 30 pounds she gained following her pregnancy and demeans her at every meal about what she is eating. He makes endless comments about her appearance and compares her in public to other women causing her great embarrassment. What is he saying? "I will love you unconditionally and completely, BUT only if you go back to looking like the woman I originally married."

Or perhaps this client I had. He and his wife had been married for seven years and she was a hoarder. One child's room was overfilled with clothes that still had price tags on them. The condition of the living and dining room made it impossible for them to entertain. Completely embarrassed by the situation, he made matters worse by demeaning his wife about the condition of the house. It was not uncommon for him to call her a slob or an unfit mother. As she put it during one session, *"he has crushed my spirit"*. He demonstrated little in the way of love because he was offended by the cluttered condition of the home.

He also had seen an attorney about a divorce and was serious about ending the marriage. When he discovered his wife was suffering from an extreme anxiety disorder and needed her own therapy, he was completely unmoved. *"She just needs to get her act together,"* he said. *"I am tired of living this way. It is embarrassing, and I deserve better. I did not sign up for this."*

He loved his wife with conditions. What he was saying was "I will love you unconditionally and completely, BUT only if you clean up this mess. I am not concerned about your mental health. My only concern is feeling comfortable in my home".

Loving with conditions is not love at all, yet in our society today, this is becoming the trend. Couples - both believers and non-believers - are running to divorce court at a rate of 50%, complaining their partner "no longer makes them happy". They equate marriage as an institution in which they measure success by asking the question "what has my spouse done for me lately". And when the answer is "not much" they see justification to pull up stakes and look elsewhere for an individual who will be more dedicated and committed to ensuring and maintaining their own happiness. That is loving with conditions. *"I will love you as long as you are making me happy. But once that changes, I am out of here."*

The Rev. Tim Keller in his book "*The Meaning of Marriage: Facing the Complexities of Commitment with the Wisdom of God*" tells us, *"...when Jesus looked down from the Cross, he didn't think, "I am giving myself to you because you are so attractive to me." No, he was in agony, and he looked down at us - denying him, abandoning him, and betraying him - and in the greatest act of love in history, he stayed. He said, "Father, forgive them, they don't know what they are doing." He loved us, not because we were lovely to him, but to make us lovely. That is why I am going to love my spouse. Speak to your heart like that, and then fulfill the promises you made on your wedding day."*

Think of loving with conditions as giving your heart to someone with a string attached. You are willing to surrender your heart, but you want something back. To obtain your love, your partner is required to provide you with something much more than simply love in return. You want a guarantee they will be devoted to making you feel content and happy at all times. And when the commitment stops – for whatever reason – the game is over. You decide to pick up our toys and find a new playmate who will agree to fulfill your commitments.

Good luck with that. Nearly 75% of second marriages and nearly 80% of third marriages end in divorce.

The God Answer to Loving with Conditions

Imagine if Jesus loved with conditions. Can you picture what may have happened at the Last Supper

"Guys, I have been thinking about it and I am just not feeling the love from the people here," he tells the Apostles. *"Even you 12 are constantly questioning me and doubting my capability. I had some big plans, but frankly, none of you deserve the sacrifice I am about to make. So, this is what I am going to do. You have 72 hours to get everyone in line singing my praises, including those folks in Nazareth. Who do they think they are anyway asking me to leave? I am their hometown boy! Anyway, you got 72 hours to help me feel unconditional love or you are on your own. And it won't be pretty – trust me."*

But that did not happen. Jesus did not always "feel the love" from the people who He came to save. But that did not stop Him from accomplishing His mission. Why? Because Jesus loves unconditionally. He refused to become offended by the insults and rejection He suffered. For Jesus, it was about the Father and us. It was not Him. Could we say the same about ourselves?

When we love with conditions, we are focused on our self-gratification. As Max Lucado would say, *"we have a problem when we think it's all about me"*. Loving with conditions is definitely "all about me".

But that is not love. Love is thinking more about someone else rather than yourself. Love is putting the needs of others in front of your own. Love does not need strings attached.

"Love must be sincere. Hate what is evil; cling to what is good. Be devoted to one another in love. Honor one another above yourselves." (Romans 12: 9-10 NIV)

Do we do this unconditionally? For the most part, no.

"For Jesus, it was about the Father and us. It was not Him.
Could we say the same about ourselves?"

Christian psychologist and author Henry Cloud described what he saw as the problem with married couples who complain things in their relationship are not fair. Cloud says playing fair is one of the surest ways to destroy any relationship. Why? *"If you treat me well, I will treat you well. That is only fair," says Cloud. "But if you treat me bad, I am going to treat you bad. It's only fair."*

Many times, when we feel we have been treated unfairly in our relationship we will use our love as a manipulative tool to cause harm. And while we may indeed hurt others, at the same time we are hurting ourselves by taking actions that cause our hearts to become more hardened.

While our human flesh makes it very difficult to love everyone unconditionally, we must work against the flesh and call out to God for the strength, energy, and patience we need to accomplish the most important of all commands.

We learn to love unconditionally when we embrace the love God has for us, while also trying to learn to love God.

"Love the Lord your God with all your heart and with all your soul and with all your strength and with all your mind; and, Love your neighbor as yourself." (Luke 10:27 NIV)

Your Roadmap to Thinking, Feeling and Acting Differently

- **Identifying Demanding Rules**

✦ Practicing Humility

1. Identifying Demanding Rules

An important step in taming the sinful desire of "Loving with Conditions" is to identify your "demanding rules." The next time you have a disagreement with your spouse or a close friend take a moment to determine if a "demanding rule" triggered the argument. If you uncover a demanding rule, ask the following questions:

1. How did this rule come to exist?
2. Am I trying to push this rule onto others?
3. How can I adjust my rule, so it does not hurt the people I love?

It is important to not dismiss the rule but instead to inquire how changes can be made among both parties to work toward an agreement. Be aware, some demanding rules are so deeply rooted having this dialogue in one sitting may not yield the answers you are seeking.

If you are the party being bombarded with demanding rules, it is important to remember these rules can be a source of anxiety to the owner. Therefore, work will need to be done to determine how to reduce the person's distress without simply giving in to their rules. If calmer heads prevail, over time, movement can be made to adjust any demanding rule that causes dissension in relationships.

2. Practicing Humility

Since becoming deeply involved in my Christian faith, I have concluded to build a strong, unwavering belief, you need a solid foundation. The first step of the foundation begins with Faith. For me, the next step should be humility. I say that because if I don't stop giving myself credit and instead give credit where it is due – to God – then everything else I set out to do as a Christian is built on a house of cards that will crumble and fall.

How can we place our trust in God if we believe we have all the answers? How do we subject ourselves to doing His work if we are self-centered and worried only about our own needs? How do we learn to love those who are unlovable if we refuse to let go of feeling offended?

When we look to stop Loving with Conditions, humility is an effective tool. When we love with conditions we are putting our needs and selfish desires before the needs of others. We are saying "your needs don't matter". There is absolutely nothing humbling about that attitude.

Humility is a choice.

"So Moses and Aaron went to Pharaoh and said to him, "This is what the LORD, the God of the Hebrews, says: 'How long will you refuse to humble yourself before me? Let my people go, so that they may worship me." (Exodus 10:3 NIV)

Pharaoh was not a humble individual (most of the kings of Egypt were not). We elect whether we wish to act with a humble heart or a hardened heart. We can begin on the path of humility when we start recognizing our own weaknesses and work to address those flaws. We also should practice going last. Instead of worrying if there will be enough for me or "will I get my share", we should stop attempting to satisfy our own needs and focus on the needs of others. And besides, we should not be concerned with our position in this world. We should be more focused on our potential positioning in the world that awaits us.

"So the last will be first, and the first will be last." (Matthew 20: 16 NIV)

Humility is difficult whether you are a believer or not. Being humble goes against our nature to obtain power and survive. But, humility lessens our anxiety by reducing our need to compare ourselves to others, while strengthening our self-worth.

Knowing we can put our needs and desires second to others warms our hearts. And that aligns us with the practice of Jesus Christ who put His needs and desires on the back burner, so we could have the opportunity to one day walk in the presence of God the Father.

"Humble yourselves under the mighty power of God, and at the right time He will lift you up in honor." (1 Peter 5:6 NIV)

CHAPTER 8: THE SHAME OF UNCONTROLLED PRIDE

"Self-centered indulgence, pride and a lack of shame over sin are now emblems of the American lifestyle." –Billy Graham

I am going to hate writing this chapter because when I think about the definition of pride, I see a photo of my face. I will admit at one point in my life, I was an egomaniac. There, I said it. As a young man, my ego was completely out of control. For Christmas one year, I gave all of my friends an autographed photo of myself (true story). In high school, I had a mirror in my locker, so when I stopped between classes, I could check out my hair.

There is nothing wrong with innocent pride. In fact, one of the definitions the Merriam-Webster Dictionary has for pride is *a feeling that you respect yourself and deserve to be respected by other people.* Now, what's wrong with that? Nothing. Having a sense that you are respected by others is healthy and allows you to develop and maintain strong self-worth.

But here's another definition of pride, also from the Merriam-Webster Dictionary: *a feeling that you are more important or better than other people.* That one doesn't sound so healthy, does it? But that was me. And it's shameful to think about.

As I got older, my pride intensified and lost its innocence. I had the answer for everyone's problem and had no issue sharing my remarkable insights. And if they did not follow my amazing words of wisdom, I would get pretty angry and tell them in no uncertain terms what fools they were. It's incredible I kept friends at all.

Because of my pride, I was forever seeking attention and needing to be noticed. I searched for the spotlight and generated opportunities to have people stroke my ego. My pride was so rampant I believed whatever I wanted or needed, I could have. After all, I deserved it.

My sole objective was to be noticed, recognized and praised on a regular basis. I believed my opinion was the only one that mattered. We needed to do things my way. And when things did not go to my liking, I made sure to wreak havoc in the lives of others around me. It was my attempt to break them down and have them do things my way. Unfortunately, it worked – a lot.

I am sad to say pride was a major factor in many poor decisions I made during the first 40 years of my life. And many of these choices caused others a great deal of anguish and emotional pain.

Shame-Filled Pride

My pride was shame-filled pride. Not because I felt ashamed of my self-absorbed attitude, but because I *should have* felt ashamed. Shame-filled pride always seeks to gratify itself. It seeks limelight, power, prestige, praise, affirmation and status.

But shame-filled pride is never satisfied. The thrill of being the center of attention lasts only if the spotlight is on. Once the light goes dark, the massive ego within begins to shrivel up, and the shame-filled individual must seek another fix to feed the unquenchable need for affirmation.

And when desire is denied, watch out! When shame-filled pride is ignored, it believes it has been disempowered. Like a child having a trauma, an individual who has shame-filled pride and believes he is losing power will turn and go to war – not battle, *war* – to become empowered once again.

While pride is a much-needed part of the human psyche, it has been responsible for much of the misery and destruction man has inflicted throughout history. Would you consider these prideful individuals?

- ☐ Napoleon
- ☐ Stalin
- ☐ Hitler
- ☐ Idi Amin
- ☐ Pol Pot
- ☐ Mao Zedong

Yes, they were prideful, but their shame-filled pride contributed to them being heartless and brutal. While the rest of the world could see shame in the behavior of these evil men, they could not see it in themselves. Why? Because their hearts were dark and hardened.

"Shame-filled pride is never satisfied and always seeks its next fix."

The basic problem with shame-filled pride is our darkened hearts. They are hearts filled with envy, hatred, suspicion, greed, anger, and most of all, fear. The fear of others discovering the intense sense of unworthiness we try to keep hidden from others and ourselves.

We see how an individual's insecurity can manifest itself into shame-filled pride when we read the story of Saul and David in 1 Samuel. Saul was selected by God as the first king of the Israelites. Soon after, God gives Saul instructions to go against the Amalekites and spare nothing.

But Saul's uncontrolled pride led him to decide he knew better than God. He went against God's commands and spared the Amalekites' king and livestock. Not one of his best ideas. From that point on it was downhill for Saul.

Reactive vs. Responsive Thinking

Shame-filled pride negatively influences our decision-making, because it drives us to make decisions based on our emotions rather than on cognitive thinking. Emotionally-based thinking is not easily subjected to rational approaches. When we are emotionally charged in our thought process, we tend to be more reactive than responsive. In being *reactive,* we simply act. It is a "Ready, *Fire*, Aim" approach. But when we are *responsive,* we first give thought to the circumstances we are facing and evaluate the pros and cons before taking action. It is more of a "Ready, Ready, *Aim*, *Aim,* Fire" approach. It's about slowing things down.

When we engage our cognitive thinking skills, we utilize the frontal cortex of our brain. When we engage in emotionally-reactive thinking, our thoughts are influenced more by the limbic system of the brain, which regulates our emotional state.

Saul relied on his limbic system for answers. Not a good choice. Then, as if things weren't bad enough between him and God, Saul decides it's time for self-promoting; so, he has a "monument created in his own honor." God has had enough. He sends Samuel to visit Saul with a rather pointed message:

"For rebellion is like the sin of divination, and arrogance like the evil of idolatry. Because you have rejected the word of the Lord, he has rejected you as king." (1 Samuel 15:23, NIV)

Ouch!

This marks the beginning of the end for Saul. God directs Samuel to select young David as Israel's next king. But Saul, instead of admitting he messed up and moving aside, continues to allow his shame-filled pride to trip him up time and time again, as he attempts to oust David.

Like Saul, when we suffer from shame-filled pride, we are lost. We are no longer the "light of the earth" because our inward focus always leads to the question – "*what's in it for me*"? We should feel ashamed for being so self-absorbed, but we don't. Not until it's too late. If left unchecked pride will be destructive to our relationships with others and with God. *"Pride goes before destruction, and a haughty spirit before a fall" (*Proverbs 16:18, NIV).

"We are no longer the "light of the earth" because our inward focus always leads to the question – what's in it for me?"

As a young adult, when I met someone for the first time, I would think to myself, *what does he/she bring to the table?* I was more concerned about what I was going to get from the relationship than what I could contribute. That was an ugly symptom of my shame-filled pride. I expected – no, make that *demanded* – people first think of what would please me. It's a sad commentary and one I hate to admit. But it was true!

I had it in my head the world and everything in it revolved around me. Why? In part, because of the isolation and abandonment I had endured as a young child and adolescent, where my primary needs for security, warmth, and acceptance were not met. As I grew older, I unconsciously set out to ensure those needs would always be met – even if it was at the expense of others. I made myself to feel entitled.

Our Shame-Filled Pride and God

Shame-filled pride can severely impact our relationship with God for many reasons. Let's focus on three.

1. When we are inflicted with shame-filled pride, we are singularly focused on fulfilling our desires. We make ourselves idols and expect God to fall in line and follow us.
2. With shame-filled pride, there is a sense that we can do no wrong. Therefore, it becomes difficult to identify and acknowledge our sinful behavior. We take on an air of self-righteousness.
3. When we are inwardly focused, we give little or no attention to others. Again, this behavior goes against the Christian life in which we are called upon to put the needs of others before ours.

It all starts with wrong priorities. Having shame-filled pride leads us to believe we are the center of our world. We know what we want and we focus on obtaining it. But that is misguided thinking. The center of our world belongs to God. Not to us. And not to our spouse, children, parents, or Labrador Retrievers (sorry Gabriel and Hunter).

The center of our world should be set aside only for God. I had a difficult time understanding this early in my Christian walk. Eventually, thanks to our merciful God, I came to understand that with Him at the center, I could be a better husband, father, neighbor, coworker, and friend. If I place myself in the center, I am working with severe limitations that will inevitably hurt all those relationships.

But God wants and deserves to be the center of our existence. When He is not placed there, He is not pleased. *"To fear the Lord is to hate evil; I hate pride and arrogance, evil behavior and perverse speech"* (Proverbs 8:13, NIV).

The antidote for shame-filled pride is humility. We build our Christian foundation on our faith in Jesus Christ. However, as I pointed out earlier, I believe the next step of the foundation must be our commitment to living a humble life. If not, everything else we add to the foundation will be weakened and when a crisis arises, it all will come crashing down.

Jesus preaches the importance of being humble, which starts with admitting we are weak and in need of God in our lives. Shame-filled pride goes against that truth. It is built on the lie that we need to rely on ourselves to manage what life throws at us. Shame-filled pride believes it is powerful when in reality it is weak. And it is that weakness we hide from the world and ourselves that we need to take to God.

"God wants and deserves to be the center of our existence.
When He is not placed there, He is not pleased."

"Each time he said, 'My grace is all you need. My power works best in weakness.' So now, I am glad to boast about my weaknesses, so that the power of Christ can work through me." (2 Corinthians 12:9, NIV

Did you catch the word *power* in that verse? God's Word tells us that by exposing our weakness to God, we receive the power of Jesus Christ working within us. If that is the case, why would we want to be in charge?

In his *Desiring God* blog, John Piper writes: *"The only road for us proud sinners to travel to reach the promised land of joy and be the free children of God passes through the valley of humiliation. It's hard and the trek requires real courage. Humbling us often feels like death, but it really is not. It's holy chemotherapy that kills the cancer of pride. 'Whoever would save his life will lose it' (Luke 9:24) means losing the 'pride of life' (1 John 2:16) in order to gain what is 'truly life'"* (1 Timothy 6:19)

The second way shame-filled pride creates a barrier between God and us is that it impedes our ability to recognize and admit our sinfulness. Shame-filled pride results in self-righteousness. We believe we are not only better and more deserving than everyone else but that we are close to perfection.

God, however, sees it a little differently.

"We are all infected and impure with sin. When we display our righteous

deeds, they are nothing but filthy rags. *Like autumn leaves, we wither and fall, and our sins sweep us away like the wind"* (Isaiah 64:6, NLT, emphasis added).

To identify and confront inappropriate thoughts, feelings and behaviors we need a softening of the heart, but that is not possible if we suffer from shame-filled pride. Therefore, we need humility in order to experience a sense of guilt over our wrong-doings, so we can take action and seek repentance. Admitting our sinfulness demonstrates humility and allows us to admit our weakness, which God finds pleasing.

"You do not delight in sacrifice, or I would bring it; you do not take pleasure in burnt offerings. My sacrifice, O God, is a broken spirit; a broken and contrite heart you, God, will not despise." (Psalm 51:16-17, NIV)

Shame-filled pride also hinders our relationship with God by requiring us to put ourselves before others. In his book *It's Not About Me,* Max Lucado describes what occurs when we are driven to focus *numero uno.*

"Self-promotion. Self-preservation. Self-centeredness," writes Lucado. *"It's all about me! They all told us it was, didn't they? Weren't we urged to look out for number one? Find our place in the sun? Make a name for ourselves? We thought self-celebration would make us happy. But what chaos this philosophy creates."*

Shame-filled pride kills relationships. And that's a problem because God is all about cultivating meaningful relationships. The individual with a shame-filled pride demeanor takes the approach he doesn't need others except to receive their praises and accolades. This individual is not concerned with the welfare of his neighbors. He is not interested in resolving social issues or concerns. He is focused on getting his needs and desires met.

This lost soul reads a verse such as, "God demonstrates His own love toward us, in that while we were yet sinners, Christ died for us" and thinks, *"well, that's nice, but it's not that important in the scheme of real life".* Obviously, he missed the following command somewhere along the way:

"Love the Lord your God with all your heart and with all your soul and with all your mind and with all your strength. The second is this: Love your neighbor as yourself. There is no commandment greater than these." (Mark 12:30-31, NIV)

Life is about relationships. The Bible is about relationships. There is no purpose without relationships. But remember, shame-filled pride kills relationships.

As I said, pride is at the top of my list of sinful behaviors. Although, after years of self-reflection, I hope my pride is more innocent in nature and not shame-filled. I believe with the help of the Holy Spirit, I have made strong strides in becoming more humble, although I am far from issuing an announcement that I am free of this sin. In fact, I realize that day will never come during my lifetime. It may be pride is my thorn and it is only by leaning on the strength of God that I have any power against this dreaded and destructive sin.

I think C.S. Lewis summed up pride well in *Mere Christianity*: *"As long as you are proud, you cannot know God. A proud man is always looking down on things and people. And, of course, as long as you are looking down, you cannot see something that is above you."*

Amen.

Your Roadmap to Thinking, Feeling and Acting Differently

- **Moving Beyond Yourself**
- **Truly Surrendering**
- **Practicing Christian Maturity**

1. Moving Beyond Yourself

Remember, it is God – and not us – that should be the center of our universe. But for that to happen we need humility. One of the issues keeping us from achieving this critical virtue is that humility is not very attractive compared to believing we are someone important and influential. But learning to move beyond ourselves and our drive for self-gratification offers rich blessings. This is known as sacrifice.

"Truly I tell you, unless you change and become like little children, you will never enter the kingdom of heaven. Therefore, whoever takes the lowly position of this child is the greatest in the kingdom of heaven. And whoever welcomes one such child in my name welcomes me." (Matthew 18:3-5, NIV)

Greatest in the kingdom of heaven. Wow, that is an impressive promise. We would be crazy not to take advantage of it. Yet, there are so many of us who keep seeking to enhance our pleasure via materialism, power, or status. We are caught up in the "I want it all" culture that surrounds us.

We measure our success based on counting the number of toys we have in comparison to others. Our warped perception is if we have more "stuff" than our neighbors, we are winning. And if we are lagging in accumulating toys, we believe we are falling behind. We have to stop believing our worth is based on material successes. We have to stop chasing toys. Our self-worth is based on our identity in Jesus Christ and is seen in the quality of relationships we formulate and maintain with Him and others.

A survival mentality (which is a "me first" attitude) is nothing more than simple-minded thinking. It limits us and our potential to accomplish all God has prepared for us to do. If I am inwardly focused, I can only engage with the limited knowledge, experience, and reasoning I have accumulated during my lifespan. However, once I move away from that limiting mindset – by turning my attention toward others – I open myself up to new learning experiences and blessings.

Instead of living in fear of one day losing everything, I now realize God's Spiritual gifts empower me to make a real difference in the lives of others. With these new gifts, I have begun to experience a profound peace about where God is leading my life. My concern no longer focuses on achieving or accumulating. God's gifts have moved my focus from acquiring more for me to providing more for others. We need to focus more on giving and less on receiving.

"We learn to measure our success based on counting the number of toys we have in comparison to others."

When we move beyond ourselves, we stop tightly clutching to false idols that bring us temporary pleasure but long-lingering grief. When we move beyond ourselves, He opens doors we never knew existed – and He closes doors such as shameful-pride that limits us in this lifetime.

"Give, and it will be given to you. A good measure, pressed down, shaken together and running over, will be poured into your lap. For with the measure you use, it will be measured to you." (Luke 6:38, NIV)

2. Truly Surrendering

I admit when I first heard about the process of surrender, I was extremely confused. From what I understood, I was supposed to give up all control of my life and hand it over to God, so He could work through me to accomplish His purposes. Give up all control? Obviously, God knew nothing about me. Control was my middle name. I loved control.

In fact, I loved control so much I not only tried to control all elements of my life, but I also attempted to control aspects of others' lives too! I thought I was very successful at it, thank you. However, I was not successful at all, because I lost many close friends who got tired of my controlling ways. In the workplace, people who reported to me quit because they were tired of trying to do everything my way.

But that didn't stop me. In fact, I never noticed I was a controlling individual. But that's what happens when you grow up in a troubled environment where things are out of control. As you grow older, you develop a subconscious mindset that says, *"the more control I have over events and people, the less likely it is that things will go wrong and cause me pain"*.

So, when I was introduced to the practice of surrender early in my Christian walk, I couldn't imagine doing it. *"I'm doing pretty well with this Christianity stuff, but surrendering? I think I will pass on that. Besides, God knows that's not my best style."*

And I was right. God did know the idea of surrender was not to my liking. What I didn't know was He didn't care. He was determined to continue to work on my transformation and He was not going to take no for an answer. I was going to surrender whether I liked it or not.

I can remember the day it happened. I fell to my knees in our walk-in closet (guess it doesn't matter where it happens as long as it happens) and I cried and cried, asking Him to take control and allow me to be *"less than the least of all His people"* (Ephesians 3:8, NLT).

That started a new chapter in my transformation. Funny thing about surrendering – at least for me – it's a process that is never completed in this life. Every time I think I've given Him every piece of me, I reach into my back pocket and find something else I'm still holding onto. So once again, I go back and surrender, asking Him to take control of another aspect of my life that if I keep holding onto will only cause me trouble.

Surrendering is a small part of you dying every day. It is what Christians refer to as being "born again." Our old self is discarded so our new self can take hold. One of my favorite Scriptures is Matthew 16:24-26 (NIV).

"Then Jesus said to his disciples, 'Whoever wants to be my disciple must deny themselves and take up their cross and follow me. For whoever wants to save their life will lose it, but whoever loses their life for me will find it. What good will it be for someone to gain the whole world, yet forfeit their soul? Or what can anyone give in exchange for their soul?'"

"Surrendering is a small part of you dying every day."

When my shame-filled pride was at its peak, there were times I felt I had a hold on the world. I was living large and doing whatever my heart desired. How that impacted others was not my concern. I thought I was in complete control. But in reality, I was out of control. While it may have looked like I had everything, I had nothing. No matter what new toy I bought, I was still miserable. I had no joy. I had no peace.

But all of that changes when you begin the process of surrender. What does that look like?

It begins when you commit to turning over everything in your life that you value more than your relationship with God. It is the process of removing false idols from your life. More specifically, it means asking the Holy Spirit to take control of how you spend your money. Requesting His help in guiding your next career move. Seeking His wisdom on how to manage your relationships. And most importantly, it is praying for Him to change – biblically circumcise – your heart, therefore, allowing you to see more clearly the ugly thoughts and feelings that dwell hidden within you.

Hidden prejudices, animosities, and even occasional warped viewpoints are destructive. They bring undue stress, anxiety and pain into our lives and the lives of others. Through humble surrender, we allow the Holy Spirit to take these harmful, worldly attitudes away and replace them with healthy, positive Christ-centered values. He infuses us with Himself. Through surrender, we stop putting trust in ourselves and instead place our trust in

God.

In surrender comes a peace and sense of freedom. We begin to recognize and appreciate our lives are now being directed by a wisdom that far surpasses our own and by a genuine love that is enormous compared to what our hardened hearts could ever deliver.

Through surrender we shed the sin of shameful-pride and replace it with the virtue of obedience to our Lord and Savior Jesus Christ – obedience to God's will that ultimately allows us to experience His joy, while comforted by an inner peace in knowing we are unconditionally loved.

3. Practicing Christian Maturity

"Be imitators of God as dearly loved children and live a life of love, just as Christ loved us and gave Himself up for us as a fragrant offering and sacrifice to God." (Ephesians 5: 1-2, NIV)

We don't like the word *sacrifice.* It brings to mind work, pain, suffering, or doing without. Can you imagine doing without? Of course not! We want what we want when we want it, right? And if we can't have it, other people will know about it.

For the most part, we are selfish people. Although we may give our time, money and skills to various charities and people in need, we are often cautious to make sure what we give does not hurt too much. Or if we are giving, someone notices. But these behaviors demonstrate a lack of Christian maturity, just like when we love with conditions.

When we accepted Jesus Christ as our Savior and Lord, we make the decision to begin the process of transformation. We recognize we were sinful creatures and it's time to exchange our old self for a new, Christ-like self. We want Jesus to take His rightful place on the throne of our hearts so we could be about His purposes.

"And Jesus came up and spoke to them, saying, 'All authority has been given to Me in heaven and on earth'" (Matthew 28:18, NIV).

That pathway is designed to help us become mature Christians. What does Christian maturity look like? It is:

- Knowing the most important relationship we have is with Jesus Christ
- Placing our trust in God and not in our own understanding
- Living in humbleness, in which we realize the benefit of being "less of the least of God's people" (Ephesians 3:8)
- Being able to freely share our testimony with others
- The ability to say no to sinful pleasures.
- Maintaining an outward focus in which we are more concerned about the needs of others.
- Being committed to spending quality time communicating with the Lord through scripture reading, prayer, and quiet time.
- Understanding and accepting that being a believer doesn't preclude us from enduring crises and hardships as a result of our fallen world.
- Forgetting what the world teaches us about values and leaning on values of the Spirit.
- Walking in faith so our Lord might demonstrate His reality in our lives.

Christian maturity is a life-long journey. And it is important to realize the path to Christian maturity will never be complete during our time in this world. As long as we inhabit these sinful bodies, it is not possible to be fully righteous in our walk with God. Our Christian maturity will only be complete upon our face-to-face meeting with Him.

"Dear friends, now we are children of God, and what we will be has not yet been made known. But we know that when He appears, we shall be like Him, for we shall see Him as He is. Everyone who has this hope in Him purifies himself, just as He is pure." (1 John 3:2–3, NIV)

What we will be, has not yet been made known.

We need to ponder those words carefully when we are flogging ourselves because we believe we are inadequate; that we don't measure up; or we are unlovable. Those negative self-descriptions have been accumulated over the years by destructive events and unsafe people who tore us down and trampled on our self-worth. Many of us spend our entire lives carrying those garbage bags, never shedding the shame labels and allowing them to keep us from achieving our full potential in Christ.

Remember, God does not see us through our eyes! He sees what He originally designed before the fallen world and evil-hearted people got their hands on us. And on the Day of Judgment, when we stand before our Lord and Savior, we will finally see what magnificent creatures we are. We will see the wonders of His works and stand in awe of the beauty and perfection the Potter created. We can't even begin to imagine what that day will be like – but we can be confident it will be the greatest moment we ever experience.

CHAPTER 9: THE SHAME OF EXCESSIVE WORRY

"My life has been filled with calamities, some of which actually happened."
–Mark Twain

You are probably wondering – is worry a sinful desire? Do people wish to worry about circumstances and people in their lives? Of course not. So then, why do we list worry as a sinful desire? It appears in this book because worry is something we indeed can influence but in many cases elect not to. And that goes against God's command to us about worrying.

"I tell you, do not worry about your life, what you eat or drink; or about your body, what you will wear. Is not life more important than food, and the body more important than clothes?" (Matthew 6:25 NIV)

Worrying (fear) is sinful because it means we are trusting in something other than God. So why don't we put our trust in God and discover we can live a more carefree life? Three reasons:

1. We neglect to turn to Him during times of crisis. He is not top-of-mind because we are too consumed with the painful circumstances we are facing and attempting to find solutions to make them go away. We are so inundated with our fears the maker of all creation becomes an afterthought to us. We find ourselves turning inward instead of outward and we believe some things are too important to give to God. We are so self-absorbed with our problems we can't recognize our real sense of comfort lies within Him.

2. We believe He doesn't care or have the time to deal with our problems. If our troubles are self-inflicted, we may believe God is ashamed and wants nothing to do with us. Or perhaps, we believe He is leaving us to clean up the mess on our own as a punishment for our mistakes. We see Him as too busy, uncaring and heartless. What we overlook is God's true feeling for each of us.

"Humble yourselves, therefore, under the mighty hand of God so that at the proper time he may exalt you, casting all your anxieties on him, because he

cares for you." (1 Peter 5:6-7 NIV)

3. We believe He can't do anything to change our circumstances. Our mindset may be God can do wonders in creating new life, but He has no clue when it comes to saving our marriages or dealing with our kids. Besides, it's complicated and only we fully understand all the details. We have the audacity to decide for ourselves what our King can and cannot do for us. Tell me that is not a sinful act?

Believe it or not, God wants you and me to have an abundant life. God does not want us living a stressful existence. He doesn't want you and I engulfed in worry. Instead, He wants us to lean on Him and accept the peace He promises.

"The thief comes only to steal and kill and destroy; I have come that they may have life, and have it more abundantly." (John 10:10 NIV)

In her book entitled, "*Since Strangling Isn't an Option*", Sandra Crowe refers to a University of Michigan study that led to some very interesting findings. It seems 60% of the things we worry (fear) about are *non-existent and irrational.* Another 20% are the fear and worry of things that have *already occurred* in our lives. 10% are *minor issues* that don't have a major impact on us. Finally, there are 10% of our worries and fears that are *rationale.*

However, what is interesting about this 10% is that 8% of it is out of our control. That leaves us with 2% of the "stuff" we worry about that we can influence. Think about it, just 2% matters.

There were similar findings in a 1990 survey by the University of Cincinnati in which researchers discovered that 85% of the things we worry about will never occur. Perhaps the famous MAD Magazine character, Alfred E. Newman knew what he was talking about when he said, "*What? Me Worry?*"

Everyone worries from time to time. It is part of our human nature. However, excessive worrying can lead to anxiety, depression, physical ailments, phobias, and isolation. Worrying also tends to magnify the situation we are facing. As I mentioned earlier, it is what I refer to as "feeding negative thoughts". A worry pops into your head and immediately you begin to expand upon it adding other negative thoughts, therefore, allowing them to swell and eventually leaving you feeling very overwhelmed.

"Everyone worries from time to time. It is part of our human nature."

How does an emotion like worry have such a strong hold on us? It comes down to our thought-process and how our brain operates. When we are deep in worry, we are engaged in a more emotionally-based thinking process. This occurs in the Limbic System of the brain, which houses the amygdala. Think of the amygdala as a thermostat that regulates our level of emotional pain and pleasure. When we are in pain - such as when we are worrying - the amygdala is extremely active.

An active amygdala requires more blood flows to the Limbic System to handle the additional workload. Where does that blood come from? I am glad you asked. It comes from the frontal cortex of the brain. And what actions do we do with the frontal cortex area of our brain?

Again, excellent question. The frontal cortex is the executor of the brain and where we do our abstract, concrete and critical thinking. When blood flows away from the frontal cortex to meet the needs of the overactive amygdala, it can cloud our judgment and reasoning.

Therefore, when we are emotionally-charged in our thinking, we are more likely to allow negative thoughts to race through our head unchecked increasing our stress level. Again, this is why we need to become more cognitive of what we are thinking throughout the day so we can capture our negative thoughts and reduce the intensity of the anxiety we are experiencing.

Basically, worrying is not only sinful, but it's irrelevant and irresponsible. It's irrelevant since most things we worry about won't happen. It is irresponsible because God is in control - whether we like it or not!

Again, it comes back to whether you accept Jesus as both your Savior and your Lord. If you see Him just as a Savior, then you will spend a great deal of your time worrying, since you have elected to take control of your life instead of putting yourself in His good hands. Those who see Jesus as both Savior and Lord understand He is the ultimate source of comfort. He is love. He is hope. He is joy.

"But you are a chosen race, a royal priesthood, a Holy nation, a people for

His own possession, that you may proclaim the excellences of Him who called you out of darkness into his marvelous light" (1 Peter 2:9 NIV).

As I mentioned earlier, there is an amazing peace and joy that comes with handing our worries over to Christ. Let's say you want to find a new job, so you begin your search. Immediately, you get a lead and interviews are scheduled. A major case of nerves develops as you begin to worry what will occur during the interview. *"What if I say something stupid? What if trip walking into the room? What if they don't like me? What if they only hire tall people?"*

Back in the 1970s, Stanley was unexpectedly called to be interviewed for a senior position in a large worldwide computer firm. He was extremely anxious about the interview and worried he would say something that would eliminate him from consideration for the job.

Having only a day to prepare he stayed up all night researching information about the company and its history. Sitting across the desk from a senior executive the next morning, anxious thoughts about messing up the interview kept running through his head. The first question was, "how old are you?". Stanley drew a blank. He was so preoccupied by worry that he could not answer a basic question. The second question was, "let's begin with what year you were born in?". After that, he settled down. Stanley did get the job.

Worrying pulls us into dark places. We become consumed trying to come up with the right answers, attire, and attitude that we should take into the interview process. But what if we handed the job search to Christ? *"Lord, You know what I am seeking, but it should be Your will and not mine. I understand if You want me to work for this company, You will open the door for me. If the door shuts, then I know I need to continue to follow our search."*

Now, the pressure is off. We do not need to worry about being perfect during the interview or even if we will get the job. Instead, we can focus our energy and efforts on preparing ourselves for the interview by researching more about the company and thinking of questions we may be asked.

With this approach, we have come into the light! When we chose to ignore Jesus as our Lord, we will be left in darkness.

Now that is something to worry about.

Your Roadmap to Thinking, Feeling and Acting Differently

- **The Worry List**
- **Putting Trust Where It Belongs (God)**
- **Turning It Into Concern**
- **Will This Matter?**

1. The Worry List

There is something amazing that happens when we take what is bouncing back and forth in our minds and put it on paper. I ask my clients suffering from excessive worry to write everything they worry about. I am quite surprised to see the length of the lists they bring back. Sometimes a client will hand in three pages of worries!

"Worrying pulls us into dark places."

When I evaluate the worry list, what we discover is similar to the findings of the University of Michigan study. A large percentage of their fears are not rational. I also find there are many things on the list the client indeed has an opportunity to change. But they have been so caught up in worrying they feel paralyzed to take action.

If you are consumed with worries, start by writing down everything that comes to mind. When you have done this, set the paper aside for a few hours and come back and analyze your list. As you walk through item by item, ask yourself the following questions:

- "Is this important?"
- "Can I change this?"

If the item is not important, spend some thinking why that's the case.

Be sure to evaluate each worrisome thought using truth and reasoning and not just your emotional-thought process. If an item is not important, put it on a separate list entitled "Does Not Matter". Once you are done creating the list, post it somewhere, so you can review it every day.

For the second question, "can I change this", evaluate each item left on your list after you remove the ones that do not matter. As you go through each worry, determine if you can take steps to change the circumstance or outcome. If not, place them on yet another list entitled "Beyond My Control". Again, place this new list next to the "Does Not Matter" list so you can review it every day. What you have left on your original list are those things you can change. Take the time to pray about them and create action steps to address them one at a time. Be careful not to attempt to tackle too many issues simultaneously. If you do, you could once again find yourself overwhelmed. Determine your priorities.

2. Putting Trust Where It Belongs

Worry is an inwardly focused activity. It fills our head with bits and pieces of a puzzle we can't put together. It's like the computer program that continues to run as it unsuccessfully looks for an answer. Worry takes us away from living in the moment and leaves our minds wandering even when we are surrounded by others. Worst of all, it siphons and drains our faith.

"We are not designed to worry," says Mitch Horton, senior pastor of Victory Church in North Carolina. *"Worry is really faith in reverse. Worry is allowing the spirit of fear to dominate and rule the situation. Fear attracts the demonic, the way that faith attracts God."*

Worry causes us to take our eyes off God, which in turn leaves us blind to the course He has established for us to move forward with our lives. Worrying leaves us in the dark searching for answers that are hard to come by, if not impossible for us to find.

A solid cure for worry is turning our focus outward and putting our trust where it belongs – in the hands of God. Instead of allowing worry to dominate our lives, we instead should be turning to Jesus to guide us.

Be in prayer on a consistent basis, asking for His strength and love. Seek wisdom from Him that can help you sort through and determine areas that you have influence over, versus those you do not. Those things in which you have influence, prayerfully act. For those elements you do not have influence over, hand them over to Jesus and ask Him for wisdom and strength to endure.

The Apostle Peter instructs us to do so, "... *Humble yourselves, therefore, under God's mighty hand, that he may lift you up in due time. Cast all your anxiety on him because he cares for you*" (1 Peter 5:7 NIV).

We humble ourselves when we admit we are weak and need His guidance and direction. We humble ourselves to trust and follow His will. We humble ourselves to keep worry in check.

"Be in prayer on a consistent basis, asking for His strength and love."

Barbara is a middle-aged woman and mother of twin boys in their late teens. Ten years ago, Barbara had a nephew who was killed in a car accident. The event caused great distress in the family and Barbara became very fearful for the safety of her children who at the time were nine. Because of her fear, Barbara micro-managed her children's lives and demanded to know where they were every minute of the day. She quit her full-time job and took a part-time one, so she could drop them off and pick them up from school every day.

As teenagers, they were restricted on where they would be and for how long. As their friends began to drive – neither of them were permitted to get driver licenses. They also were forbidden to take rides from friends. Of course, this led to greater stress in the household, but Barbara did not care since her only concern was in keeping her unrealistic fears under control.

When the twins headed off to college they rebelled against their mother's domineering style and started to withdraw from her. This caused even greater anxiety for Barbara who would call or text the twins 40-75 times a day. Most of the time they ignored her attempts to connect, only adding to her anxiety.

In working with Barbara, I needed to help her understand there are some things she could not control. And if she insisted on trying, she would only continue to subject herself to extreme anxiety and drive her boys further away.

Barbara had spent years trying to contain her sons in a plastic bubble due to the misplaced trust she put in herself to be responsible for that role. At some point, when the boys started to mature, she needed to let them experience things on their own and make mistakes, which in turn would have served as growth experiences for them.

Instead of continuing to put her trust in herself to ensure the safety of her sons – which they would no longer allow her to do – Barbara needed to learn to put their safety at the feet of Jesus. During months of therapy, Barbara eventually saw the benefit of leaning on Jesus to care for her sons. She came to understand her worrying did nothing to protect her boys, but only drove a wedge between her relationships with them. Although her newfound trust in Christ did not guarantee something bad could not happen to her sons, it did mean Barbara could be at peace in knowing that whatever happened to them, Jesus was part of their lives.

As we review our worries, we should make it a habit each day to ask God, *"what is it I should focus on today?"* Listening to Him in silence will help us map out our course each day and provide us with a plate that is not too overloaded. We should act on the items He directs us to respond to and lay aside at His feet the rest of our worries for another day.

3. Turning It Into Concern

As mentioned before, excessive worry is a self-indulgent activity. Even if you are worrying about a friend or family member, you must be cautious not to take your negative-thought process to the extreme. How do you accomplish this? You turn your worry into concern.

There is a major difference between worry – which we have described as unproductive speculation of events that most likely will never occur – and concern. Concern is the ability to assess the situation, which in some cases can lead to problem-solving. There is no problem solving associated with worrying. When we are concerned, we are drawing God into the mix.

Suppose it is a Saturday morning and you discover a lump on the side of your neck. Worrying will take you down the path of assuming the worst and dialogue that may sound like this *"Of my gosh! What in the world is this? I bet its cancer! I can't believe I have cancer! My grandmother died of cancer. It must be cancer. I am too young to die!"*

...we should make it a habit each day to ask God,
"what is it I should focus on today"?

Concern will take you down the path of rational thinking that may go something like this, *"There is nothing I can do about it at the moment. I hope it is nothing serious, but I will call the doctor on Monday and schedule an appointment. No sense assuming this is serious. I think I will take a moment and pray about this".*

"Don't fret or worry. Instead of worrying, pray. Let petitions and praises shape your worries into prayers, letting God know your concerns. Before you know it, a sense of God's wholeness, everything coming together for good, will come and settle you down. It's wonderful what happens when Christ displaces worry at the center of your life." (Philippians 4:6-7 NIV)

If you do not believe there is a BIG difference between worrying and concern – think again. It can make all the difference in the world how well you sleep.

4. Will This Matter?

Another helpful technique to combat excessive worrying is to ask yourself this simple question, "will this situation still be a concern in a week, a month, or a year from now?" In a majority of cases, you will find the answer is "no." Because we are so emotionally-based in our thinking during times of worry, we tend to overstate the severity of the situation. This then inflames the intensity by dwelling on negative thoughts instead of attempting to process the situation rationally. By learning to evaluate the relevance of your worries and putting them to reason and logic, you will gain a great advantage over them. This new freedom will empower you to improve the quality of your life.

When it comes to worry, our problem is we fear an invisible future that a timeless God has seen. Perhaps you should talk to Him about it.

CHAPTER 10: THE SHAME OF SELF-LOATHING

"When we don't know who to hate, we hate ourselves."

–Chuck Palahniuk, American Novelist

Sarah was a 22-year-old who came to see me after returning from a year-long mission assignment in South America, where she worked with orphan children. Since her return, she had been struggling to adjust to life back home and was fearful she no longer had a purpose. At first, this seemed like a normal case of adjustment disorder, but as we continued to meet, it turned out Sarah was not suffering from an adjustment disorder but instead was struggling with extreme low self-worth.

During our third session in which she was describing her daily activities, she blurted out "I hate myself!" Through more investigation, I would soon find a young woman who felt worthless, ashamed and bent on self-destruction. For more than six months, she had been cutting herself and engaging in promiscuous sex in an attempt to deal with the uncontrollable emotional distress she was enduring. With this destructive behavior came enormous shame and guilt, which only served to feed her self-loathing.

As a counselor, I have come to realize a common denominator many clients have is they think poorly of themselves. In fact, many – like Sarah – hate themselves. They wear negative labels such as: failure, loser, misfit, outcast, pathetic, and freak. They perceive themselves as inadequate compared to others and being of no value to anyone. The internal self-talk they launch at themselves day in and day out goes beyond negative and approaches the level of vile.

"If you had a person in your life treating you the way you treat yourself, you would have gotten rid of them a long time ago," is how Cheri Huber, author of "*There is Nothing Wrong with You: Going Beyond Self-Hate*" describes self-

loathing individuals.

Where does this sense of self-loathing develop? In many cases, it is associated with abuse in childhood where constant criticism and emotional trauma were the norm. This could include parents, relatives, peers, or other authority figures who:

- Rarely provided praise but were quick to point out faults and shortcomings
- Engaged in verbal abuse and name calling such as: loser, stupid, ugly, fat, etc.
- Showed no affection or sense of caring, therefore giving the impression of rejection
- Gave the message of being disappointed by negatively comparing the child to others
- Devalued a child through harmful actions and words
- Were absent as the child was growing up. They may have been physically present but emotionally, they are not available

This type of abuse doesn't have to happen in the home. I would estimate more than 80% of the individuals I have worked with who suffered from anxiety and depression endured severe bullying at the hands of their peers or siblings. It is a stream of continuous teasing, mocking, and rejection that leads the victim to wonder "what is wrong with me".

Being ego-centric, children believe they are responsible for what happens around them. Therefore, the on-going criticism and abuse they face cause them to believe they are bad and unlovable. Their mindset is – if they were good children, their parents, siblings, peers and others would heap upon them praise instead of negativity and abuse. Children will ask, *"what have I done that they don't like/love me?"* or *"why am I so different than everyone else that I do not belong?"*.

Nearly all trauma leads to the development of poor self-worth that plays itself out in negative thinking, emotions, and behaviors. It is through those poor behaviors the idea of being a "bad" person is reinforced and more firmly entrenched. As the child moves into adolescence, teenage years, and adulthood, this way of thinking becomes ingrained in their soul.

If self-loathing is something that is created due to trauma, how is it a sinful desire? It is sinful because as adults, there is something we can do about it.

As children, we don't have the thinking capacity to figure out the real problem is not us. Instead, it is the result of the neurosis of others who are supposed to be caring for us, or heartless peers. But as adults, we have the capability of processing the negative thoughts we have about ourselves and correcting them. We can take the question, "what is wrong with me?" and hold it up to the mirror of logic and reasoning. If we do, we would understand our beliefs that we are worthless, undesirable, and unlovable are nothing more than lies.

"...we elect to stay stuck in our negative-thought cycle and end up remaining a shame victim."

But instead, we elect to stay stuck in our negative-thought cycle and end up remaining a shame victim. Self-loathing is a sinful desire because we allow ourselves to stay immersed in an internal cesspool and make little effort to reclaim the identity that is ours, being defined in Jesus Christ. We refuse to take the steps necessary to strip away the shame and embark on a new journey that will allow us to live an abundant life. We continue to believe the lies. But we are wrong. As a child of God, we are indeed significant despite our emotional scars.

"Until our hearts find complete security and significance in God's unconditional love, we will never be satisfied," says Rene Swope, author and co-host, of Proverbs 31 Ministries.

Imagine a life in which there is no sense of satisfaction. Is that what God wants for you and me? Did He create us, so we could live a life full of torment and disappointments? No, He did not. Your Father in Heaven loves you and me. He doesn't want us flogging ourselves. He wants us to break the chains of guilt and shame, so we can know and experience unconditional loved and acceptance.

The time to change is now.

Your Roadmap to Thinking, Feeling and Acting Differently

- **Understanding How God Sees You**
- **Ending the Negative Self Talk**
- **Embracing Emotional Pain**
- **Forgiving Yourself**

1. Understanding How God See You

While we may feel broken – and we are – we need to remember as Christians, we are beautiful in His eyes. The problem most of us endure is we believe He sees us as we see ourselves. If we believe we are worthless and unlovable, we will assume God feels the same about us. But that is not the case.

"For you created my inward being; you knit me together in my mother's womb. I praise you because I am fearfully and wonderfully made; your works are wonderful, I know that full well. My frame was not hidden from you when I was made in the secret place, when I was woven together in the depths of the earth." (Psalm 139: 13-15)

How comforting it is to know God views us as He designed us. That was before others got their hands on us and played havoc by hard-wiring our brains and emotions. That was before the fallen world cursed us with disease and deformities. No, God sees us in a way we have never seen ourselves, nor that we can ever imagine. I often wonder what will it be like on judgment day when I stand in front of Him with Jesus at my side and I see for the first time how He created me. I can't even begin to imagine what that will be like because it is far too much for my puny brain to comprehend.

"Dear friends, now we are children of God, and what we will be has not yet been made known. But we know that when Christ appears, we shall be like him, for we shall see Him as He is." (1 John 3:2 NIV)

But sometimes having the insight that God loves us unconditionally is not enough to break free from the shame we feel. These toxic emotions make it difficult for us to approach Him. But what is ironic is God sees our brokenness and understands our shame. Once again let's look at Psalm 139 for the truth.

"If I say, "Surely the darkness will hide me and the light become night around me, even the darkness will not be dark to you; the night will shine like

the day, for darkness is as light to you." (Psalm 139: 11-12 NIV)

God tries to explain to us – *"do not be afraid to approach Me with your shame. You try to keep it in the dark away from Me, but that is not possible because I know your shame and I will bring it into the light. Bring your shame to me, not so that I can condemn you, but so that I can remove it from you".*

This is a powerful message for those who believe God can never accept them because of their sinful behaviors. But once again, the idea that God is unapproachable and uncaring is nothing more than Satan's lies designed to drive a wedge between God and us.

Try this exercise. Go to a quiet place where you will not be disturbed. Close your eyes and imagine yourself in God's presence. Hear Him call your name and tell you how much He loves you. Then imagine Him placing His arms around you and holding you in a loving embrace. Feel the love God has in His heart for you. Listen to His voice as He asks you to tell Him how you are feeling. Talk to Him as you would a close and intimate friend who you trust. If you struggle at first, don't give up. Go back the next day and try again. And again. And again. With perseverance, it will take hold.

As we discussed in Chapter 2, our sense of significance, which means "I am valued, wanted and accepted," can be delivered on a consistent basis through only one source – God. God loves you unconditionally and always will. His love for you never changes.

"For great is His love toward us, and the faithfulness of the LORD endures forever. Praise the LORD" (Psalm 117:2 NIV)

Remember this – you are the prince or princess of a King. Now, doesn't that make you feel special?

2. Ending the Negative Self-Talk

Although we discussed negative self-talk earlier, it's worth repeating since it is the core of many of our emotional issues.

The first step in alleviating negative self-talk is becoming aware it's there. Negative self-talk is so destructive because it can manifest itself with a single negative thought. That one thought can get the anxiety train racing and before we know it, we are an emotional wreck. By being cognitive of our thought process, we can capture negative thoughts and deal with them before they get out of control. It is important to remember we control our thoughts, emotions, and behaviors.

*"We are destroying speculations and every lofty thing raised up against the knowledge of God, and we are taking every thought captive to the obedience of Christ." (*2 Corinthians 10:5 NIV)

"By being cognitive of our thought process, we can capture negative thoughts and deal with them before they get out of control."

Once we have identified our negative thinking, we must discern to determine what thoughts are based on truth and logic and which ones are the results of emotionally-charged thinking. This is not always easy to do, especially when we are in a highly-charged emotional state. We must first relax by using breathing and mindfulness techniques that have been suggested throughout this book.

After calming ourselves, we then can take our negative thoughts and look at them through the lens of rational thinking and truth. With this new focus, we can begin to understand what we can influence and what we can't influence.

We can take charge of what we need to take action on. What we can't influence, we lay at the feet of Jesus. Let's look at an example.

Judy is extremely angry with herself. She went out drinking last night and ended up sleeping with a strange man. Here is her internal dialogue. *"What the hell is wrong with you? Do you have no morals? You are so disgusting. You're a pig and you make me sick."* Her verbal attack leads her to take a razor and cut herself to inflict self-punishment for her actions.

Where should Judy have taken the negative thought "what the hell is wrong with you" before she allows it to manifest itself out of control? Here is one option.

"What the hell is wrong with you? Well, I know something is wrong with me. First, I can feel all this tension in my stomach and shoulders. I need to relax. Let me take a few minutes to breathe and focus on getting my head cleared."

After calming herself down and praying for truth, Judy could go to the next step of managing her negative thinking. *"I can't understand why I keep making the same mistakes repeatedly. It's not like I enjoy giving my body away.*

And I know how I will feel once it's over. I can't allow this to make me feel like a bad person. But I also need to take action to determine why I do what I do. Lord guide me. I think I will call a psychologist to get an evaluation."

Removing herself from highly-charged emotional thinking allowed Judy to think more clearly and make a rational decision regarding her situation. It also stopped her from beating herself up and escalating the situation to where she would act out and physically harm herself.

What Judy did was quiet her critical inner voice. This begins by first becoming aware of the destructive thoughts that play repeatedly in your head. It's the small recording tape in the back of our brain that never shuts off. It can serve as an endless sense of torment. The key to stopping the tape is to first be aware it's playing.

This is not always easy because we have been conditioned to allow the tape to play. Once we are aware of the negative messages that ramble through our minds, we can learn how to dispose of them. How? Stop feeding them.

These messages are similar to a fantasy that starts with one thought or image but manifests as we fuel it with additional thoughts and ideas. I tell my clients to externalize the negative thought. They are instructed to pretend they can see the thought in front of them and tell the thought *"I will not feed you"*. Then they are to focus on something else and allow the thought to go hungry and fade. If it comes back – and at the beginning of this process the thoughts return frequently – they are instructed to continue the dialogue with the thought. *"So I see you have come back. Well, I still will not feed you. I am going to ignore you because you are nothing but a lie."*

At this point, my client is instructed to once again return to another activity. As you continue to work on learning to dispose of your negative thoughts, you will discover you have more power over your negative thinking than you ever imagine.

3. Embracing Emotional Pain

Moving forward, we must identify defense mechanisms that have developed to cope with the emotional pain we have been carrying all of these years. Some of us learned to isolate ourselves to avoid close relationships. Others maintain an exhausting schedule of activities that keep them focused on everything except their suppressed emotional turmoil. Yet others turn to destructive addictive behaviors. The path we select doesn't matter, what does matter is our ability not to identify or engage with the emotional pain.

Whatever defense mechanisms we put in place as a child or adolescent must be removed as we learn to accept and cope with our emotional distress in healthy ways.

This may sound crazy, but when we ignore our emotional pain, we need to find ways to distract ourselves. Some of the outlets we select are not healthy and can become addictive. The problem with addictive behaviors is they serve as a stop-gap and only temporarily hide our emotional pain. Once the addictive distraction is over the emotional turmoil starts again.

The healthy approach is to accept and embrace our emotional pain. We need to learn to be able to sit with it and endure it. What this will teach us is the pain, while discomforting, will not kill us. We will live to see another day. That does not mean we like the pain or welcome it, but that it is not bigger than us. It does not define who we are. Most importantly, we will no longer allow it to direct our lives.

As we go through this process of coping with emotional distress, after a period of time we will find ourselves feeling "tired." That indicates we have dealt with the pain well and it is time to put it aside for a while. We then go on and function in healthy ways until the pain reappears and we repeat the process. What we are learning to do is grieve. If we do not grieve losses and disappointments, they will haunt us. Our emotional pain, if not dealt with properly, will serve as a cancer in our lives that can lead to more distressful emotions including resentment and bitterness.

Another helpful aspect of learning to cope with your emotional pain is that it provides us with an opportunity to learn more about ourselves. Growing mentally, emotionally, and Spiritually is a cornerstone of the Christian life. We should constantly be seeking to identify how we are falling short in our walk with Christ and find ways to allow Him to strengthen us. However, it is very difficult to grow stronger when things are going well in our lives. We have more opportunity to grow stronger during these painful times.

"Growing mentally, emotionally, and Spiritually
is a cornerstone of the Christian life."

As we process our emotional pain, we should be asking "what am I learning about myself from all of this suffering". We may discover a personality flaw, or we may come to understand that we have weak boundaries when it comes to engaging with others. Our reflection may help us realize in the future that we need to place more of our trust in God. There are numerous things we can learn about ourselves during those stormy times in our lives. We limit our understanding when we don't spend time learning how to deal with our emotional pain.

How long will you need to endure the hurting? That depends on the offense. The more traumatic the event, the longer the healing process takes. But notice the key word in that last sentence – healing. That is what occurs when God shares His Spiritual truth and you learn how to deal with your emotional pain in a healthy way. You heal.

4. Forgiving Yourself

For those individuals who are riddled with self-loathing, the thought of forgiving themselves is not on their radar. But self-forgiveness is a critical step in tearing down the wall of self-hate.

When we don't accept and forgive ourselves for past sins, we are entering into conflict with God. For the actions Jesus Christ took on the Cross led to the forgiveness of our sins. Whether we like it or not, that is the truth. The sins of our past, present and future have been washed away by the blood of the Lamb. God forgives us.

Yet, despite knowing this fact, some continue to carry the garbage bag of shame and regret throughout their life. They engage in eternal flogging because of their sinful actions. But ask yourself this question. If we refuse to accept that God has forgiven us, are we not saying that Christ came and died for nothing?

C.S. Lewis said, *"If God forgives us we must forgive ourselves otherwise it is like setting up ourselves as a higher tribunal than Him."*

Who are we to believe our sins are greater than the sacrifice made by the only pure and innocent man who ever walked the face of this earth? Who are we to question God, who is able to forgive us what we cannot forgive in others? Who are we to question our creator? Who are we to question our Heavenly Father?

How does a person begin the process of self-forgiveness? First, you need to understand when it comes to your sins God has "moved on." He is not focused on your sinful past. As far as He is concerned, if you have repented of your sins, it has been granted.

"And no longer shall each one teach his neighbor and each his brother, saying, Know the Lord, for they shall all know me, from the least of them to the greatest, declares the Lord. For I will forgive their iniquity, and I will remember their sin no more." (Jeremiah 31: 34 NIV)

Start down the path of self-forgiveness by writing a letter to God. In this letter, outline your emotional pain. Describe to Him the destructive thoughts and behaviors that have resulted from this pain. Tell Him your struggles to forgive yourself. Describe why you feel stuck and alone. Let Him know how you long to be accepted and loved and ask for Him to guide and nurture you.

We also learn to forgive ourselves when we move the focus from ourselves and turn it outward toward others. Self-loathing is like a crutch, it requires individuals to live in misery and focus on their own issues. This usually results in isolation and it is a dark and lonely place. However, there is no need to stay stuck in the loneliness and sadness Satan uses to hold you captive. Instead, you need to reach out and see how you can assist someone else. By doing so, you are saying "no" to Satan and refuse to continue to be enslaved by him. Instead, you are shifting your focus, recognizing you are a special child of the King.

It is important to know we can go home – and God is waiting with open arms for us. Our living God is here to ensure we have hope and success in breaking the cycle of shame.

CHAPTER 11: THE SHAME OF A HARDENED HEART

"If you can't do great things, Mother Teresa used to say, do little things with great love. If you can't do them with great love, do them with a little love. If you can't do them with a little love, do them anyway."

–John Ortberg

"What's in it for me?" That was a driving force in everything and with everyone I interacted with for the first 40 years of my life. Before I would engage, I wanted to know what I was going to get for my efforts. And when I felt the return-on-investment wasn't high enough, I would not engage. I would turn and walk away. I could easily shut people out of my life if I felt they brought no value to me. You see, I suffered from a hardened heart.

I cannot tell you how difficult it is to write those words, but they are true. I suffered from a hardened heart. Losing a father at the age of 5; having a mother who endured multiple mental breakdowns; and having been shipped out several times to relatives I barely knew before age 7, led to the development of a hardened heart.

The messages I received indirectly by these early events in my life were, "people you love will leave you" and "people who love you are not reliable". Carrying those messages with me as I became an adolescent, teenager and adult meant I would need to be guarded when it came to relationships. My defense mechanism was "one foot in and one foot out". I never knew how to fully commit to anyone. And I didn't. I had people thinking they were involved in secure and enduring relationships when it was nothing but a house of cards.

Please understand, none of this was a conscious effort on my part. This was a coping mechanism I developed as a child and it was utilized without being cognitive of the thinking and feelings behind my actions. That does not excuse my behavior or the behavior of millions who act similarly. What I should have done once I saw the destructive effects of my behavior on others was to seek help to determine why I acted in such a hurtful way.

A hardened heart is usually generated via the result of abuse and neglect. These individuals once put their faith in someone(s) who violated their trust. This in turn, makes them leery when openly giving their hearts to others. This type of trauma doesn't only occur when we are children. There are many people who grow up in loving and secure homes but experience devastating emotional trauma as adults that results in the drying up of their hearts.

"A hardened heart is usually generated via the result of abuse and neglect."

Individuals suffering from a hardened heart are limited in how much emotional intimacy they can give and receive. This is because they fear being hurt again. They quickly learn how to navigate through the paths of a relationship and give just enough love and attention to keep their partner engaged. However, over time their partner becomes disappointed by the lack of emotional intimacy – then issues begin to develop.

What's important to realize is many individuals suffering from a hardened heart want to engage in relationships, but they are too obsessed with their fear of abandonment or mistrust. This makes it is impossible for them to be vulnerable and open with others.

A hardened heart shuts down others, while developing numerous techniques to keep people at arm's-length. One way is by limiting communication, especially emotionally intimate conversation. They also may monopolize conversations; talk over others who are speaking; or be short and dismissive in their answers.

Bonhoeffer saw this behavior in his Christian brothers and sisters. *"There is a kind of listening with half an ear that presumes already to know what the other person has to say. It is an impatient, inattentive listening that despises the brother and is only waiting for a chance to speak and thus, gets rid of the other person."*

One of my clients labeled poor communication skills as *"mis-underlistening"*. Personally, I think that sums up the communication styles of many couples I have met over the years! They are trying to shut their partner down because of their own discomfort in being emotionally vulnerable.

"One of my clients labeled poor communication skills as mis-underlistening."

Another negative result of a hardened heart is it can lead to our insensitivity toward sin. When we possess the worldview that people are not emotionally safe, we develop an attitude of looking out for ourselves. We believe others will not nurture or care for us. Therefore, we must be on the alert to obtain nurturing wherever we can get it and in whatever form it is available.

That may mean being sexually promiscuous, emotionally manipulative, or greedy. It is an *"anyone for themselves"* mentality. This results in insensitivity toward the needs of others, as well as not caring about what is right and wrong.

"Having lost all sensitivity, they have given themselves over to sensuality so as to indulge in every kind of impurity, and they are full of greed." (Ephesians 4:19 NIV)

Living with a hardened heart is lonely, even if you are surrounded by "loved ones" because you never fully allow people into your life. Your fear of abandonment requires you keep everyone at a safe distance. You may give the impression that you're engaging and enjoying relationships, but people seldom get to experience the vulnerable side of you. You lack the ability to share on an emotionally-intimate level. In fact, you may have a difficult time identifying any emotion that goes beyond angry, sad, happy and scared. Your worldview of not sharing emotions helps to keep you isolated and safe. The belief is *"sharing emotions is not a good thing"*.

Individuals with hardened hearts have a fear of allowing people to get too close for they may see their vulnerability. These individuals believe "when people get too close, you are giving them the power to inflict emotional pain." By never becoming fully emotionally attached, they believe they are protecting themselves from potential heartache. The other fear that prevents a hardened heart from allowing others to get close is, *"if they see the real me they will be disgusted and reject me".*

People with hardened hearts do not trust others and they do not trust God. They develop a false reality, believing those who love them are responsible for broken dreams and promises. The mindset of the hardened heart individual is, *"if those who love me can't be trusted, how can I possibly put my trust in God, especially when He allowed the traumatic betrayals to happen".*

But the hardened heart is blind. Its focus is internal, and it works to convince individuals they will forever be victims. But by limiting their emotional response and forming venues of isolation, these individuals are being cheated out of living an abundant life. They experience an emptiness and internal void that feels like they are dragging a 10-ton boulder.

"People with hardened hearts do not trust others and they do not trust God."

What the person with the hardened heart does not understand is, if they turn to God for assistance, their heart can be melted.

"I will give you a new heart and put a new Spirit in you; I will remove from you your heart of stone and give you a heart of flesh." (Ezekiel 36:26 NIV)

God has the capability of restoring our ability to love others and allow ourselves to be loved. He is the author of love and can soften our hearts and help us place our emphasis outwardly.

"Beloved, let us love one another, for love is from God; and everyone who loves is born of God and knows God. The one who does not love does not know God, for God is love." (I John 4:7-8 NIV)

Remember the verse from Romans 5:5 that we shared earlier?

"More than that, we rejoice in our sufferings, knowing that suffering

produces endurance, and endurance produces character, and character produces hope, and hope does not put us to shame, because God's love has been poured into our hearts through the Holy Spirit who has been given to us." (Romans 5:3-5 ESV)

God's love is in our hearts. Tapping into the Holy Spirit is one of the first steps to warming the hardened heart.

Your Roadmap to Thinking, Feeling and Acting Differently

- **Allowing God to Nurture You**
- **Learning to Nurture Yourself**
- **Taking a Chance on Others**

1. Allowing God to Nurture You

When we suffer from a hardened heart, we need to learn how to love again, and for some, perhaps for the first time. Although it is not impossible, sometimes it is very difficult to do. Along with our lack of trust in people's ability to love us unconditionally, we also don't know how to identify safe, loving people who we can become emotionally vulnerable.

So, what source can we turn to learn to love? How about to source and the greatest provider of love available – God! No one can love like God loves. In fact, we can't quite comprehend God's love.

- He loves us despite our lack of love toward Him
- He sent His Only Son to die for our sins, so we can one day walk in His presence
- His desire is for us to love our enemy and pray for those who persecute us

This is a love only God can produce. Unlike God, we can't imagine loving those who ignore us. Or loving those who hurt us. Or loving those who defy us. Or loving those who put other things and people before us. No, this is a crazy love.

In his book *Crazy Love*, Pastor Francis Chen says this about God's love.

"The fact is, I need God to help me love God. And if I need His help to love Him, a perfect being, I definitely need His help to love other, fault-filled humans."

Since God is the only true and ultimate source of love, we should turn our hardened hearts toward Him and let him melt them by nurturing us. God is the ultimate nurturer. He is in the business of transforming hearts. As the creator of all things, He understands what it is like to comfort and cultivate His creations. And we are His finest creations. We are His children and He loves us unconditionally. He wants us to experience the reality of His love and He offers to nurture us in that love.

"God is the ultimate nurturer."

---

*"As one whom his mother comforts, so I will comfort you; you shall be comforted in Jerusalem." (*Isaiah 66:13)

When you come to experience His amazing love, you will develop a sense that you can handle anything the world throws at you. You also will experience the softening of that hardened heart. Turn to your Father and ask for His guidance and power to share and receive emotional intimacy. You will benefit greatly from experiencing some crazy love.

Let's face it – no one loves like God does.

2. Learning to Nurture Yourself

In most cases, individuals with hardened hearts did not receive a great deal of nurturing as a child, adolescent or teenager. They also have a difficult time identifying and expressing their emotions beyond anger, happiness, and sadness. As we begin God's process of softening our hardened hearts, it is helpful to learn how to nurture ourselves.

Self-nurturing is a skill we learn when raised in a secure and loving environment. As children, our Godly caregivers teach us how to calm down when we are emotionally distressed. We self-sooth by utilizing one or more of our five senses. Spend time evaluating when you are upset. Which of your five senses can you engage that helps you calm down?

For example, I prefer touch. If you go through our home, you will find soft, cozy fleece blankets in many of our rooms, including on our bed. You see, I love the feel of a soft blanket against my face. Obviously, you have figured out I was a child raised with a blanky. What a horrible day it was when mom took my blanky away. But that is another story.

For some, their sense of hearing can provide comfort through listening to music or sitting outside and hearing the sounds of nature. Others prefer utilizing their vision and may find looking at a painting, reading or watching a comedy can be soothing. The same holds true to our sense of smell (aromatherapy is an example) and taste (herbal teas). The key is discovering the sense or senses that help you experience comfort in challenging times.

3. Take a Chance on Others

There is no doubt a person in your past has hurt you. And in some cases, hurt you badly. But that doesn't mean you quit. Quitting may seem like it is protecting you from emotional harm, but what it is doing is keeping you a captured victim.

As you allow yourself to be nurtured by God, you also should be in constant prayer with Him asking to bring into your life good, healthy and safe people who will show you genuine love. And when these people start to appear, you should not be afraid to "go slow". You don't have to jump into the deep end of the pool. But instead, you can take your time and share small pieces of your emotional self. Test them to see if they are indeed safe. And when they pass the test, give them another test. Hopefully, over time they will prove themselves trustworthy and you will know the experience of enjoying healthy relationships.

While it is not a guarantee everyone you find in a church is "safe," it is probably not a bad place to start your journey in learning to trust. Look for a small group or Bible study that is established and start there. You also may want to explore Emotional Anonymous, which is a support group for those who struggle in sharing their feelings with others.

ABOUT THE AUTHOR

Eddie Capparucci is certified as a licensed professional counselor by the State of Georgia. He is a member of the American Counseling Association, American Association of Christian Counselors, and the Georgia Licensed Professional Counselors Association.

Eddie has a private practice in Marietta, GA, where he and his wife, Teri, have committed themselves to helping others understand the truth of God's love. They work primarily with individuals and couples who are dealing with the destructive aftermaths of sexual addiction.

Among his many clients have been National Football League and Major League Baseball players. He is certified in sexual addiction by the International Association of Certified Sexual Addiction Specialists and the American Association of Christian Counselors.

He is a clinical contributor for the National Decency Coalition, an organization designed to encourage and assist policy makers and government authorities to enforce current obscenity laws, create new obscenity laws that reflect declining trends, and take real action toward the 'health crisis' of pornography.

He graduated with High Distinction from Liberty University in Lynchburg, VA with a master's degree in counseling. He also serves as an elder at Eastminster Presbyterian Church in Marietta, GA.

He and his wife have two children – a daughter, Chelsea and a son, Dakota. They also are the proud owners of two very spoiled Labrador Retrievers.

REFERENCES

Arterburn, Stephen and Stoeker, Fred. *Every Man's Battle.* Waterbrook Press. 2000.

Bevere, John. The Bait of Satan. Charisma House, Lake Mary, FL. 1994.

Bonhoeffer Dietrich. Life Together: The Classic Exploration of Faith in Community. Harper Collins Publishers, NY, NY. 1954.

Bradshaw, John. *The Shame that Binds You.* Health Communications Inc. Deerfield Beach, FL. 1988.

Chen, Francis. *Crazy Love*. David C. Cook Publishing, Colorado Springs, CO. 2013.

Crabb, Larry. *Effective Biblical Counseling*. Zondervan Publishers. 1977.

Crowe, Sandra. *Since Strangling Isn't an Option.* Penguin Group. New York, NY. 1999.

Dyer, Wayne. *The Power of Intention: Learning to Co-Create Your World Your Way.* Hay House Inc. 2010.

Ellis, Albert. *Overcoming Destructive Beliefs, Feelings, and Behaviors.* Prometheus Books, Amherst, NY. 2001.

Forward, Susan. *Men Who Hate Women and The Women Who Love Them*. Bantam Books, NY, NY 1986.

Huber, Cheri. *There is Nothing Wrong with You: Going Beyond Self-Hate.* Keep It Simple Books, 1993.

Jennings, Timothy. *Could It Be This Simple?* Lennox Publishing. 2012.

Jones, Robert D., *Redeeming the Bad Memories of Your Past Sins.* The Journal of Biblical Counseling, Fall 2003.

Keller, Timothy. The Meaning of Marriage: Facing the Complexities of Commitment with the Wisdom of God. Riverhead Book, NY, NY. 2011.

Kendrick, Stephen. The Love Dare. BH Publishing Group, Nashville, TN. 2008.

Lucado, Max. *It's Not About Me*. Thomas Nelson Publishing. 2004.

Lewis, C.S. *Collected Works of C. S. Lewis*. Thomas Nelson Publishing. 1996.

Lewis, C. S. *Collected Letters of C. S. Lewis*. Thomas Nelson Publishing 2006.

Lewis, C.S. *Mere Christianity.* C.S. Lewis Pte. Ltd. 1952

Maxwell, John. *Be a People Person.* David C. Cook, Colorado Springs, CO. 2007.

Mentor, Jeanette Elisabeth. *You're Not Crazy – You're Codependent*. J2 Publications. 2011.

Ortberg, John. The Me I Want to Be: Becoming God's Best Version of You. Zondervan, Grand Rapids, MI. 2010.

Tozer, A.W. *The Pursuit of God.* Christian Publications, Harrisburg, PA. 1950.

Schnarch, David. *Passionate Marriage: Keeping Love and Intimacy Alive in Committed Relationship*. W. W. Norton & Company. 2009.

Swindoll, Chuck. *Day By Day*. Thomas Nelson Publishers, NYC, NY. 2000.

Warren, Rick. *The Purpose Driven Life.* Zondervan, Grand Rapids, MI. 2002.

White, Ellen. *Fundamentals of Christian Education.* Ellen G. White Estate. 2010.

Wright, Norman H. *Making Peace With Your Past.* Revell Publishing. Grand Rapids, MI. 1985

Yerkovich, Milan and Kay. *How We Love*. Waterbrook Press, Colorado Springs, CO. 2008.

CPSIA information can be obtained
at www.ICGtesting.com
Printed in the USA
BVHW01s2306210118
505484BV00007B/46/P

9 781684 330102